A Strega's Grimoire:

The Rituals

A Strega's Grimoire:

The Rituals

Patricia Della-Piana

This compilation of a lifetime's work is devotedly dedicated to Marla, who carries the torch.

© 2010 Patricia Della-Piana

All rights reserved, including the right of reproduction, in whole or in part, except for private study, research, criticism or reviews. No part of this book may be reproduced without prior written permission. Inquiries should be made to the author, at deliathecrone@yahoo.com.

Cover embraces the art work of Leandro Della Piana © 2010
Art work on page 90 is by Patricia Della-Piana, © 1997
Published in the United States by Lulu.com

A Strega's Grimoire: The Rituals
by Patricia Della-Piana
ISBN 978-1-257-84563-7

"Ritual is the way you carry the presence of the sacred. Ritual is the spark that must not go out."

Christina Baldwin, author, speaker, educator; founder of PeerSpirit; co-developer of From the Four Directions

Introduction

The word 'ritual' comes to us from the Latin, *ritualis*, a version of the base word, *ritus*, which means rite. It was first noted in common use around 1560 or 1570, in the Old French language. Rituals were always symbolic and highly personal, created especially to trigger responses that would affect the spirit of all participants. In the middle ages, the Protestant Reformists were vigorous in removing every trace of the occult, of magic or any ritualization from their religious practice. Their meeting houses were barren of figurines, statues or even paintings; "holy" water wasn't used; and ordinary bread and wine or water were consumed in place of the "blessed host" previously offered, which were not considered to be a spiritual transubstantiation of the deity's body or blood, but were consumed in remembrance of the deity instead. In these and many other examples you can see how all sense of ritual was quite neatly removed from religion.

Ritual serves many purposes in our lives, offering comfort, support, healing, control, self-assurance, camaraderie and connection, in an otherwise singular and solitary existence. Claude Lévi-Strauss (1908-2009) said, in 1981, that ritual "turns back towards reality" in that "it is not a direct response to the world, or even to experience of the world; it is a response to the way man thinks of the world." We use ritual to remind ourselves of the inner meaning of life, and as an invitation to the reality of ourselves. The goal of any ritual, therefore, is to seek beyond it for a deeper meaning, for there is something wise, honest, adjustable and real behind each ritual we perform.

Over the years, I've been honored to be asked to create rituals for great occasions in the lives of my friends and acquaintances. Each time, I'm happy to report, the ritual was a considerable success and was enjoyed by all the participants.

Every ritual was written either for a specific individual's event, or for a gathering of goddess people of all traditions. Because of these restrictions, each ritual contains characteristics of various belief systems, seasoned with my own spiritual poetry. I attempted to write rituals that would be as non-committal as possible to any particular tradition, which would still embrace the needs of the participants who would be present.

As a spiritual poet, I must admit that much of what I write is meant to touch the reader (or, in the case of ritual, the performer) deeply, generating outward signs of emotion. Don't be afraid to let those feelings show. They are an honest way to present your emotions to the other participants, letting them know that you feel the same way they do, which doubles the relation and fellowship of the ritual. Performed superficially, rituals are superficial, but, performed with genuine devotion, a ritual can be truly transformative. They are as relevant to our lives as we allow them to be.

The individuals for whom some of the rituals were written were kind enough to permit me to include their personal ritual in this collection. However, I have removed all names and/or other identifying information.

You may notice that some of these rituals appear to have been written for a female-only gathering. That's because some of them were. If this is not appropriate for your group, small changes can be made to convert those rituals for a more co-ed group, and accommodate your needs.

In no way do I wish to give the impression that any of these rituals is the *only* or the *correct* or even the *most spiritual* way to perform them. They are simply the way I chose to produce them, at the time I wrote them, for the purpose they were written. If you find any portion of them to be worthy of incorporation into your own ritual, I am doubly honored.

Table of Contents

Section I	*Solar Rituals*	1
Chapter 1	*La Vigilia*; known in other traditions as Yule or Winter Solstice	3
Chapter 2	*Lupercalia*; known mundanely as Valentine's Day	14
Chapter 3	*Primavera Giornata*; otherwise known as Spring Equinox	22
Chapter 4	*Calendimaggio*; also known as Beltane	29
Chapter 5	*L'ore d'Estate*; otherwise known as Summer Solstice Rituals	35
Chapter 6	*La Giornata della Dea*, or Goddess Day Ritual	51
Chapter 7	*Abbondanza!*; otherwise known as Fall Equinox	60
Chapter 8	*Il Viaggio delle Morte*; known in other traditions as Samhain and a short ritual	64
Section II	*Rites of Passage*	74
Chapter 9	Dedication	76
Chapter 10	Initiation	85
Chapter 11	Welcoming; known in some areas as Wiccaning, or Witchering	91

Chapter 12	House Blessing 105
Chapter 13	Croning 109
Chapter 14	Witch's Tea 118
Chapter 15	Wise Resolutions 124
Chapter 16	Womantide, a Menarche ritual 132
Chapter 17	Shadowland Ritual 141
Chapter 18	Handfastings 147

Section III *Lunar Rituals* 178

| Chapter 17 | Romancing the Moon, a Full Moon ritual .... 178 |
| Chapter 18 | Drawing Down the Crone, a New Moon ritual .... 186 |

| Appendices | .... 193 |
| Index | .... 211 |

Solar Rituals

The Sabbats originally represented the changes in the agricultural year, including planting, tending crops and harvesting. As such, they were all based upon solar dates. Although farmers still use these dates in pretty much the same ways, most of today's population is not involved in the agriculture business, so the schedule is more or less out of touch for the modern pagan.

In the Stregherian tradition, witches do not use the word Sabbat for their seasonal rites. They use the word *treguenda* (tray-gwen-dah), and they state that it means 'quarterly or every three months'. (However, the word, in Italian, for 'quarterly' is *trimestrale*.) There is an Italian word *tregenda*, which, in some Italian/English Dictionaries, means 'witches' sabbath', but it also means 'pandemonium'. Interesting?

The members of that tradition celebrate eight *treguendas*: four major and four minor. The major, or Spiritual, festivals occur in October, February, May and August. The minor, or Earth, festivals occur on the Spring and Autumn Equinox and on the Summer and Winter Solstice.

My particular practice does not recognize many of the *tregendas* mentioned above, but eight *Sabbati*, nonetheless. Here you will find the rituals I've written for those annual festivals, all of which I consider to be both spiritual and earthly. They occur in December, February, March, May, June, August, September and October. The actual dates, along with the rituals included, are listed below:

La Vigilia (The Vigil) December 21
Lupercalia (Festival of the Wolf) February 15
Primavera Giornata (Spring Day) March 21
Calendimaggio (First Day of May) May 1
L'ore d'Estate (The Hours of Summer) June 21
      and Summerfest, a Fairy Ritual June 21
La Giornata della Dea (The Day of the Goddess) August 13-15
Abbondanza! (Abundance!) September 21
Il Viaggio della Morte (The Journey of Death) October 31
      and Shadowfest, Feast of the Ancestors (a solitary ritual) October 31

The names by which I know these Sabbats are derived from my own heritage, and perhaps result from the ancient practices in the area of Abruzzo, where my own Italian ancestry began. Some of the rituals are much longer than the simple one-to-three hour events so common among some groups. In fact, two of my rituals take several hours, from sunset to sunrise, and from sunrise to sunset.

I'm fairly certain your path will not match mine, but I hope you will find these Sabbat rituals to your liking, enough that you will be able to incorporate bits and pieces of them into your own rituals for these times of the year.

La Vigilia

(The Vigil) or, Winter Solstice

A 12-hour vigil, to be held on December 21

In ancient Mesopotamia (modern Iraq), people celebrated 12 full days of the Winter Solstice, believing that the sun, which had become cold and distant, unable to foster the growth of crops, would never return to the earth unless they were to honor it, celebrate it, and sacrifice to it. The ancient Egyptians had pretty much the same idea, celebrating the creation of the universe and the birth of the Sun god, Ra, for 12 full days. These were rituals of renewal, in which chanting, fasting, bells, feasting, candles, incense, and holy waters were used. Even the ancient Celts celebrated and sacrificed for 12 full days, believing that the Cailleach (the crone) and her icy fingers had gripped them tightly, because the sun was standing still for all of those 12 days, and only their worship would loosen her grip and allow the sun to move again. The Norse tradition lasted a full twelve days of celebration, with bonfires to burn away the old year and welcome the brightness of the new year.

The Scots left us a nursery rhyme titled, "The 13 Days of Yule", in which a king presents a flurry of gifts to his beloved over the extended celebration. The gifts include 8 different kinds of birds, 3 different beasts, one human and one plant. This rhyme was probably the incentive for our modern "Twelve Days of Christmas" song, but the king did not present his gifts in the amounts mentioned in the modern song. Instead, most gifts are given in groups of three – a magic number, of course – and only four of them are given singly. Should you wish to somehow incorporate the Scottish gifts into your Yule, the gifts were, in order, a papingoe (peacock), 3 partridges, 3 plovers, a grey goose, 3 starlings, 3 goldspinks (goldfinches), a brown bull, 3 ducks laying, 3 swans swimming, an Arabian baboon, 3 hounds hunting, 3 maids dancing and 3 stalks of corn.

Our ritual cannot cover a 12-day period, unless it would be an expensive, expansive affair which includes overnight facilities and meals. So we will compress the twelve days into the twelve hours of the longest night of the year, the night before Winter Solstice. In my Italian-American family, we named the Christian holiday *La Vigilia*, the vigil, and that's how I wish to celebrate it here, in a raw pagan form.

A large red candle is lighted at the beginning of each hour, and snuffed at the end of each hour – not blown out. If you are unable to locate a candle that will burn for twelve hours, you could substitute twelve red candles that will each burn for one hour. If the candles don't burn all the way out, save the stubs to melt down into another large candle, as the stubs, having been burnt in the circle are now instilled with divine energy and should not be wasted. The stubs could also be distributed to the participants for their own melting into a new candle.

The nine-foot wide circle is protected with bits of holly, whose prickly edges prevent evil spirits from passing through.

The first hour begins at sunset the night before the solstice. Some years, this is December 20, while other years, it might be as late as December 23.

This is a time to bid goodbye to the old year, and the old sun; to honor the darkness; to consider the losses of the past year, and reflect on the coming year. Traditionally, the first day (or night) of Yule was called Mother Night, in which contact with spirits and ones' ancestors was made.

The litany of the year is intoned at this hour, with 12 readers, or as many as you have, taking turns. If you have more than 12 people to read, choose just twelve, one for each month.

Jangle the bells to waken the crone as she nods
Febrile in her dotage, yet crafty and wise
Marvel at her ability to stand with the gods
Apraxia be damned, the old year swiftly flies
Mayhem reigns as the people grow impatient
Juno bids us lay aside our grievances now
(Juleps could be served to minimize dissent)
Auguries abound, seeking still her weary brow
Separate the darkness of winter from the light of spring
Octaves of praise and poem fill the universe
Novel as the warmth is, let it glow with the new king
Decree the year at ending, for better or worse.

(Alternatively, a guided consideration of each month could take place, with everyone having an opportunity to relate their memories – pleasant or not - of that month, briefly.)

So ends the first hour.

The second hour is a Silent Hour, spent in meditation, or in journalizing one's thoughts of the past year or the coming year. Have paper, blank books, pens and pencils available for any who need them. The appropriate garb would be black robes, as black celebrates the darkness, heightens emotional responses and grounds the wearer.

This will be the longest and most difficult hour of the entire vigil.

Absolute silence must prevail this hour, no music, no speaking.

Small slips of paper could be offered for each participant to write something they wish to remove from their life (a memory, a habit, etc.) and these papers will later be burned.

So ends the second hour.

The third hour is the Hour of Air, which will be spent with music, bull roarers, bells on ankles and wrists, windchimes, rattles, etc.

Participants are masked, and are led in a labyrinth dance or procession, happily, but not hysterically. The masks, which were brought to the festival by each participant, can represent a favorite god or goddess, or any of the usual characters seen during the Winter Solstice, including Santa, Father Time, elves, the horned god, the Greenman, etc. The labyrinth represents the path that has brought them to this point and the path that lies ahead. A simple labyrinth pattern painted on a sheet of canvas can be laid in the center of the circle for the purpose of the dance, and removed when the dance has ended.

A fire is lit, but is not permitted to become a blazing fire, just something warm to light the circle.

So ends the third hour.

The fourth hour is the Hour of Touch. Participants are given bits of earthen clay or other modeling material, with which they will either make a figure for their own nativity of the sun, a figure for the group's *crèche*, or they will add their bit to the others' bits to create a cave for the group's *presepio*.

A drummer could play in the background, softly, or you can have a mechanical music player with recorded seasonal music.

During this hour, participants can fill the time by telling of the blessings which befell them over the past year, having dispensed with any difficulties or problems during the second hour. This discussion should be positive in tone, and uplifting for everyone.

So ends the fourth hour.

The fifth hour is the Hour of Earth, in which participants will dress the Yule tree, which is the tree of memory, surrounded by a small circle of plain stones. Lights, ornaments, garlands, etc., can be added to the tree, along with a goddess or a star at the top. Participants could bring prepared ornaments specifically meant for the group tree, or they could make simple ones, like paper snowflakes or stars, if you care to supply craft materials for that purpose. Remember to keep this activity to one hour only!

If the tree is outside, let the decorations be for the animals who will come across it – birds, squirrels, etc. Pine cones spread with peanut butter and rolled in birdseed, apples, nuts, etc., can all be added to the woodland tree, along with strings of popped corn, cranberries, and the like.

Pagan carols can be played or sung or both during this hour.

So ends the fifth hour.

The sixth hour is the Hour of Taste. Now is the time for the sacred meal, the cakes and ale portion of the ritual. In Italy, one of the traditional 'meals' provided for guests during this season is roasted chestnuts and sweet wine, which would make for an interesting sacred meal. Another Italian possibility is *bruschetta*, freshly-baked bread slathered with the best olive oil you can manage, and Strega, the liqueur created by witches in Benevento. Let the hour begin with the preparation of the sacred meal, as you have determined it should be, leading up to the actual partaking of it at the end of the hour.

A special blessing is repeated to each guest, as the food and drink are passed:

May you always have enough, and some to share
May you always have a voice to raise in prayer.

Bell music should prevail during this hour, or you might continue with the pagan carols.

So ends the sixth hour.

The seventh hour is the Hour of Water, in which ice figures or snowmen are considered to be the divine victims. Ice figures can be made in the household freezer, in shaped molds, and will melt slowly during the hour, especially if placed near candles, or the fireplace.

The song, "Frosty the Snowman" could be sung and the participants told that this children's favorite actually tells the tale of a 'person' who is simplistically sacrificed (by melting) to be reborn when the snow falls again. Historically, the divine victim is either a king, a chief or a deity, or he may be a delegated substitute for that leader. Such a leader must, of course, be strong, fearless and fertile, to bring such qualities to his devotees. When he begins to show signs of aging or infertility, he is sacrificed for the good of his charges, in order that a young and fertile leader take his place. This kind of sacrifice is still being performed in some parts of the world today, although it is usually a ritual only, and no actual death occurs in these modern times. Ice figures can be flavored frozen pops (like popsicles) in the shape of men and women on a stick, for the participants to eat, thereby consuming the sacrificed victim.

Rain sticks should be the musical instrument this hour, mimicking the sound of melting snow and ice.

So ends the seventh hour.

The eighth hour is the Hour of Smell, when colored and scented veils are wafted by dancers who entertain those not dancing. The dancers are decorating the ribbon tree of hope (a la Maypole). If veils cannot be found, colored and scented ribbons can be used, if long and floaty enough to do the job. The ribbons can be used alone or attached to sticks which allow them to waft more delicately. Ribbon colors and their correspondences can be seen on the Notes page, at the end of this chapter.

Music is provided by flutes.

So ends the eighth hour.

The ninth hour is the Hour of Fire, as the dancing becomes ecstatic. Obviously, the black robes are put off for the purpose of dance, revealing the yellow gown beneath. This can be covered or accented with scarves or veils of other bright colors, according to each dancer. A color chart accompanies this page, for information. The dancing takes place around both trees that have been decorated – the Yule tree of memory and the ribbon tree of hope. Music is whatever seems appropriate for the dancing.

This is also the time to burn the scraps of paper written out in the second hour. Perhaps the dance could signify the freedom one experiences once the negative aspect is burn and lifted. In that case, a participant would approach the fire, and burn the paper prepared in the second hour, then turn away and begin to dance.

The fire, which has been tended carefully all these hours, is now stoked and fed to create a strong, blazing fire.

So ends the ninth hour.

The tenth hour is the Hour of Sight, when divination of all types take place. Mirrors are available for scrying, space is provided for tarot readings, etc.

Music is from any string instrument, like guitars, harps, etc.

Santa, the original winter shaman, can be present at these activities. The Celtic traditions hold that the Holly King, representing the old year, dresses in red, and drives a team of eight deer, which sounds a lot like our jolly old elf.

Gifts can be exchanged at this hour, in the name and memory of departed loved ones, perhaps accompanying a mention of why that departed one is still so beloved, or was so, when alive.

So ends the tenth hour.

The eleventh hour is the Hour of Spirit, as the Nativity of the Sun is completed. The figures are placed in the cave, while the goddess, clad in a starry garment, is carried seven times around the circle in her delivery process, and a drum is sounded throughout. If the journey of the goddess is acted out by real people, the group's maiden should play the part of the goddess, and she might even walk or ride around the circle rather than be carried, if that is a problem. This can also be enacted by carrying a decorated statue around the circle.

The litany of the 13 moons is read aloud, either by one person, or by 13 separate people. Our Litany is based upon the First Nation names for the moons.

The Wolf moon howled so hungry at the door
Cold and lonely, it longed for the fire's roar.
The Snow moon blanketed the land again
As all that's left for man to eat is grain.
The Crow moon called to us and just in time
To say that winter's o'er and so the rime.
The Fish moon swam the skies to spawn anew
The wheel it turned for me and also you.
The Flower moon it blossomed all around
To please the eye and nourish all the ground.
The Rosey moon brought thorns and sometimes tears
And now the longest day of all appears.
The Thunder moon roared all across the sky
Yet even then the land was high and dry.
The Red moon glowed at rising in the eve
And smiled on us as we brought in the sheave.
The Corn moon stalked us in the ripened field
And waved silky beams across the season's yield.
The Harvest moon enlightened all the land
And gave its power to help us understand.
The Frosty moon just glistened over all
As, aging, it shone on us, great and small.
The Cold moon shivered as it rose at last
To end the cycle, joining those that passed.

A modern birthing ritual can be enacted, with a masked male, representing the Sun, crawling between the opened legs of all the women in the circle. Chanting can accompany his journey, as you deem appropriate.

So ends the eleventh hour.

The twelfth hour is the Hour of Sunrise, when we greet the new Sun, and celebrate the rebirth of the light. Dancing and celebratory activities prevail, and the music is of any kind that pleases the participants, and encourages them to dance, but bells should ring to herald the arrival of the newly-born Sun.

At this hour, the black robes would be shed, revealing the glorious shades of yellow and gold gowns worn beneath, to welcome the new Sun.

The fire, if it has not gone out by now, is put out, with respect. Bits of the ashes are distributed to each participant for their own use, as they represent the sacrifice, hopes and celebration of the group, and bring good fortune, placed upon a personal altar, or worn in a locket.

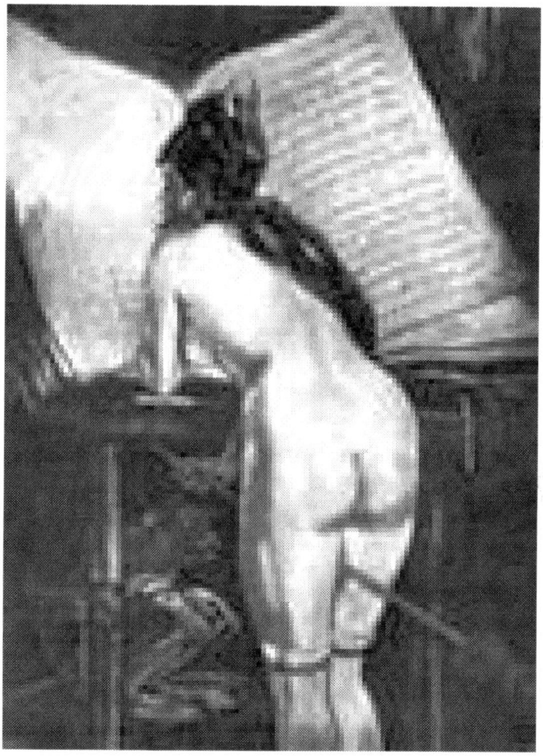

Lupercalia

This is a nine-hour ritual, honoring the ancient celebration, which spanned nine days. The purpose of *Lupercalia* was to celebrate and generate human fertility. It is to be performed on February 15.

The first hour, which begins around 3 o'clock in the afternoon, is for crafts. The group will gather at tables where undecorated masks are available, or each participant could bring his or her own mask to complete here. Offered for the use of all are paints, beads, feathers, stick-on jewels, fast-drying *papier mâché*, and any other decorative materials you feel are appropriate to create a mask to save as a remembrance.

The masks can be of animals, mythological creatures, deities, or any other form that pleases the wearers. Have suggestive pictures at the ready for your guests' inspiration.

The second hour is an hour of renewal. For this entire hour, you will decide:
You might choose to renew your pagan dedication

You might want to renew your vow to your chosen deity

You might wish to renew yourself, for instance, from a fearful (sedentary, debt-ridden, lonely, unhealthy) person to a courageous (active, financially-secure, outgoing, healthy) one. Perhaps you have become lax in regard to your original intentions. Perhaps you've allowed other things to prevent you from realizing those intentions.

In that case... renewal can be a difficult process, as you must clear away everything that stands between you and success. Don't believe that this exercise is going to be a breeze, since it only lasts one hour. If you have more to work on than can be covered during the hour, this will be only the gateway for your journey. But journey you must. Divine energy will move your mind and your body, freeing you, by making you aware of how you harm yourself (if you do), so you can stop. The spiritual energy unleashed by this process will wash your mind clean, but it can bring great sadness along the way, resulting in the renewal you seek. The process might also bring intense pleasure as you journey. Each person will travel in their own manner, as their needs demand

Here is an idea to jump-start your renewal process:

A) Write out on paper the part of your being that you want to remove: like loneliness, financial struggle, unhappy relationship, etc. Write the details of why this needs to be gone from your life, and get detailed in your writing. This might result in painful memories or thoughts arising, attempting to turn you back against this course of action, but you must persist. If you truly wish to overcome this problem, you must persist. When you have written as much as you can, take the paper to the altar and offer it to the deity as a sacrifice, while you burn it in the cauldron of renewal. Watch it burn, knowing that the difficulty is leaving your consciousness as it dissembles.

B) Then go back to the writing area, take another paper, and begin to write what will take the place of such obstacles. You must complete both parts of this journey, for you have removed a part of your psyche, and the void must be filled with something. It is now up to you to make that something a positive influence on your spirit. Remember, however, that this is a journey; whatever you write will affect your life from this moment, and could cause you a different set of miseries than the original problem did. It is an adjustment. Your process may take you places you hadn't expected. When you have written a detailed example of what will take the place of your problem, bring it to the altar, and lay it at the feet of the image of deity there. Offer this gift as proof of your dedication to renewal.

C) When the offer is completed, join your sisters and brothers in a joyful grounding, by dancing, eating, laughing and embracing the changes that are about to happen in each of you.

If your group is small enough, you might consider allowing one person at a time to approach the altar and complete the work needed to be done there, until all have had an opportunity to renew. They will all come together in joyful celebration when every one has completed their journey. If one or more people seem to have extreme difficulty with the first step (or even the second), let the other members of the group be as supportive as the sufferer needs them to be.

The third hour is for love divinations and fertility spells. Tarot cards and tables to spread them on should be available, as well as areas for

astrological work, pendulum work, scrying and the reading of tea leaves.

The fourth hour is for crafts once more, when the group will gather to create a riding horse, much like the old stick horse of one's childhood. Of course, your riding beast can be a wolf instead of a horse, in keeping with today's ritual. A participant can bring her or his own completed beast, if preferred, but you should provide sticks (at least 5-feet long), socks for the head (can be brown, tan, black, white, or a combination of any colors), buttons or jewels for the eyes, yarn for the mane, strips of leather or leather-like material for the reins, felt for the ears or teeth, and any other materials that seem to fit the occasion.

The fifth hour is the hour of the King. A king of the *Lupercalia* is to be chosen and crowned as such, by whatever means you determine are appropriate for your group. This could be based upon what the participant is wearing, or how well he has created his crafts. You might also have a dance competition between all the men attending, and choose your king as the winner of the contest, according to the will of those being entertained. Of course, if there is only one male, or masculine personage, present, that person will be crowned king. It is hoped that you will have several male or masculine persons to choose from, allowing a fun competition for everyone.

The crown you choose can be as simple or as decorative as you wish. It could be simply a hat, decorated light-heartedly for the event. It could be entwined herbs, or even folded paper. At the end of this book is a page showing how to create a simple folded-paper crown. The king will also need to carry a crook, which is simply a stick with a curved top, rather like a plain cane, which could suffice. An oversized candy cane could be used, or shepherd's hook meant for the garden. The hooked stick is an ancient symbol of renewal.

The sixth hour is the feast, in which the king should be served first. If you started the ritual at 3:00, it is now 8 o'clock in the evening.

The feast, for *Lupercalia*, should consist mostly of meats and wine. In ancient times, the meat was sacrificed especially for this feast. If, in these modern times, you are unable to sacrifice your own meats and you wish to be certain that your meats retain that pure, sacrificial aspect, you might consider purchasing kosher meats. I suggest marinated meats be cut into small chunks and cooked on skewers, so they might even be eaten with the hands, as the *Lupercalia* is also a celebration of the wildness of human nature. Small potatoes can be added to the skewers, if desired. Plenty of bread should be offered. At some point, a decadent dessert can be offered, like a chocolate souffle. Indulgence, and even over-indulgence, is to be encouraged here.

The cooking of the meats can be included in this hour, provided the cooking and eating can be accomplished within the one-hour time allotted. If you choose to have the foods eaten with the hands, be sure to supply scented, wet towels for clean-up afterward. An appropriate scent would be marjoram.

The seventh hour is a quiet time for all, in which a pagan drama play will entertain everyone. In ancient times, dramas were an important part of the festivities, and you might want to have one of your group write a short play just for this occasion. The theme of the play should be fertility, birth and/or celebration, and the tone could be rowdy, if your participants are all adults. If you include children in your celebration, be aware of what is included in the drama play on their behalf. Alternatively, you could use any of the dramas listed at the end of this book.

Young children could be dismissed at the end of the drama, because the remainder of it can be a little much for the little ones.

The eighth hour is the hour of purification, which was the purpose of the ancient ritual. It begins with the sacred meal, the cakes and ale, blessed and distributed according to your group's tradition.

Then the king will 'purify' each masked person in the circle, according to their wishes, either by a touch, a kiss or by three gentle strokes with a soft whip. The whip should be scented with either Patchouli or Ylang Ylang.

The purification is hoped to bring fertility to the receiver, either in body, in spirit, or in mind. Let the whipping honor the receiver's wish; for instance, if the receiver wants fertility in body, as for conception, the stroke should be at the lower torso. Fertility of spirit can be a stroke on the heart, etc. Each participant will take their purification in turn, then cavort about the circle on their horse, until all have been purified and are a-gallop, and the king is able to join the dancers.

Let this be a pleasant dance experience, building into a more riotous performance at the ninth and final hour.

The ninth hour is the Dance of the Wolves, when the dancing between the participants becomes more personal, and more intense. It is suggested that each female in the circle dance especially for the king, and then for any other male (or female) in the circle to arouse them. By this time of the evening, the time should be midnight, and any very young children will have retired so that the adults may perform this portion of the ritual without concern. Don't be surprised if you hear the howling of wolves!

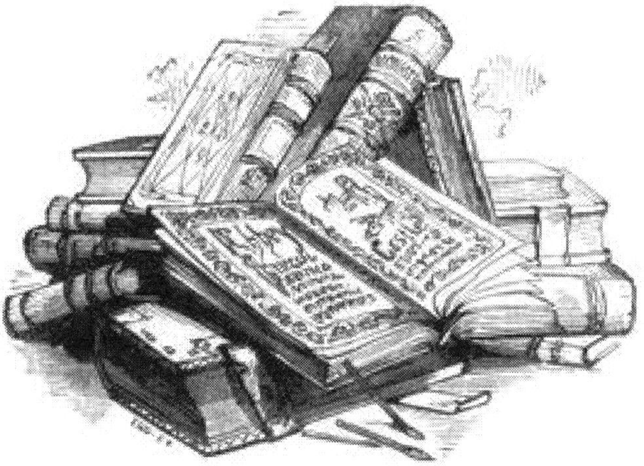

Primavera Giornata

a Spring Equinox Ritual

This ritual was performed on March 21, 2004

Invite all within the circle

Sweep the circle:

The Priest/ess intones:
"*As I mark the circle round,*
all within are loving bound,
all without are held apart,
now we ply the witch's art."

Call the Elements

At the Eastern point of the circle, a chosen worshiper calls:
"*Wind swirls potential around us,*
increasing our anticipation,
heightening our imagination,
swelling wonder in our minds.
By Her breath that is the air,
we summon elements of the east to participate here.
Hail and Welcome!"

At the Southern point of the circle, a chosen worshiper calls:
"*Warmth radiates throughout our circle,*
igniting our excitement,
expanding our courage,
shaping our fervor.
By Her passion that is the fire,
we call elements of the south to share our sacred space.
Hail and Welcome!"

At the Western point of the circle, a chosen worshiper calls:
"*Water's tranquility soothes us,*
holds us in Her embrace,
streams through our dreams,

surges our compassion.
By Her womb that is the water,
we summon elements of the west to accompany us.
Hail and Welcome!"

At the Northern point of the circle, a chosen worshiper calls:
"*We feel the earth firm under our feet,*
strengthening and grounding us,
embodying our creativity.
By Her body that is the earth,
we call elements of the north to partake of this moment.
Hail and Welcome!"

Call the Deities

The Priest, in the center of the circle, calls:
"*We seek the god and goddess eternal,*
the divine energy internal;
we desire the presence of truth.
We call upon the power of spirit to enter and fulfill us here and now. Welcome Home!"

The Priestess, in the center of the circle, calls:
"*We are within sacred space, where none have been before, and all have been forever. So mote it be!"*

Preparation of the guests for the Sacred Union

The Mother, traveling deosil around the circle, anoints each worshiper with oil, welcoming them to the celebration, saying:
"*This is the time of awakening, that all the universe awaits,*
Attend to this holy union, and bless it with your energy."

The Maiden, bearing blessed and salted water in an asperger, travels deosil around the circle, sprinkles each guest, saying:
"Begin the sacred journey, receive the waters of rebirth.
Give your self to us, give your spirit to Earth."

The Crone, bearing towels for drying, should anyone need one, travels deosil around the circle, announcing to each guest:
"Now comes the virgin goddess, willing, inspired.
Now also comes the god, the love desired."

The Great Rite

The Priest, enacting the role of the god, stands in the center of the circle, saying:
"The nubile goddess awaits her impregnation of life. She is weary of the long, cold winter, when she lay alone, with only a promise to cherish. I have come to adore her, and restore her passion in my own. For I am the seed, hungry for the womb."

The Priestess, enacting the role of the goddess, joins the god in the center of the circle, saying:
"Here at last is my salvation. Here is the spark that will bring me to my fullness. His is the power I have desired, the energy I have needed. I have loved him once, and I love him still; I always have, and I always will. Come, Beloved, penetrate the earth with your spirit. Enter the goddess with joy."

At this point, the priest and priestess enact the Great Rite, in whatever manner is appropriate for your tradition.

Celebration of the Union

A boisterous celebration ensues.

The worshipers engage in a celebratory dance, around the circle, with each other, and with the priestess and the priest, if they are able to join the worshipers. All participants of the dance are to demonstrate their ecstasy at the union of the God and Goddess, in whatever manner is appropriate for your tradition.

The Sacred Meal

The Priest offers the bread, saying:
"Bless this bread which is filled with the power of your fruitfulness. It is made from the wheat that grows in your fields, water from your springs, and the gift of yeast from your loving heart.
**Make this bread nourish the faith of each who eat of it.
So may it be."**

The Priestess passes her hand over the bread, enacting a blessing. She then takes a bit from the loaf to feed the earth, another to feed the Priest and one to feed herself. The Priest then distributes the loaf to the worshipers, saying:
"Never hunger."

The blessed bread is offered and distributed to the participants, in like manner.

The Priestess offers the wine, saying:
"Bless this wine which is filled with your spirit of celebration.
**It is made from the grapes that grow on your vine, sweetness from the kiss of your light, and the gift of yeast from your loving heart.
Make this wine nourish the passions of each who drink of it.
So may it be."**

The Priest passes his hand over the wine, enacting a blessing. He then drops a sip from the chalice to quench the earth, offers a sip to the Priestess, then takes one himself. The Priestess then distributes the wine to the worshipers, saying:

"Never thirst."

The blessed wine is offered and distributed to the participants, in like manner.

Now the circle closure begins, in the opposite direction that the circle was opened.

At the Northern point of the circle, a worshiper calls:
"Thank you, earthen elements of the north, for partaking of our moment.
We release you now to your fertile realm.
Hail and Farewell!"

At the Western point of the circle, a worshiper calls:
"Thank you, watery elements of the west, for accompanying us.
We release you now to your loving realm.
Hail and Farewell!"

At the Southern point of the circle, a worshiper calls:
"Thank you, fiery elements of the south, for sharing our sacred space.
We release you now to your passionate realm.
Hail and Farewell!"

At the Eastern point of the circle, a worshiper calls:
"Thank you, airy elements of the east, for participating here.
We release you now to your wondrous realm.
Hail and Farewell!"

Dismiss the deities

The Crone, in the center of the circle, says:
"Thank you, God and Goddess, for including us in your joyous union."

The Maiden, in the center of the circle, says:

"The circle is our sanctuary; it is always open, always yours."

The Mother, in the center of the circle, says:
"We release you now to your glorious realm. Hail and Farewell!"

Dismiss the Guests

Priest:
"Merry Meet"

Priestess:
"Merry Part"

Priest and Priestess, together:
"And Merry Meet again!"

Calendimaggio

May Day

Calendimaggio is the Italian word for 'first day of May', which refers back to the Latin *calend,* meaning 'first', and the Italian *di maggio*, which means 'of May'. In many of today's pagan traditions, the first day of May is celebrated as Beltane, Walpurgis Day, Rowan Witch Day, Tanith's Day, Floralia, Rodonitsa, or Mayday. It is one of the very important sabbats of the solar calendar, being the polar opposite of Samhain, and the only other time that the veil between the worlds is thin enough to permit messages to pass between them.

May Day is unique, in that it is the only pagan festival that wasn't adapted by the church for its own use, or given a Christian name or purpose. As such, much of the traditional activity of this sabbat is considered to be un-Christian or distasteful, even in today's world.

One of the most common practices on this sabbat is the erection and dancing about the Maypole. In some places, the Maypole is exactly that - a pole - erected in a central area, decorated with flowers and ribbons for the purpose of dancing. In others, a living tree is hewn, erected and decorated. In Italy, the Maypole is called *l'Alberi della Cuccagna,* which means 'the trees from the land of milk and honey', and is actually a greased pole, upon which a prize is placed, and the first person to climb the pole, get the prize and return safely to the earth with it, is chosen King (or Queen) of the May. This ritual will employ a more traditional use of the Maypole, and one that is ecologically sound.

You will need a potted living tree, large enough to dance around yet small enough to be carried into the temple and placed at its center.

You will also need:
many decorations deemed suitable for a spring festival
floral garlands to decorate the outer edges of the temple
   baskets of flowers that can be strewn across the temple floor
a special floral wreath/circlet for the 'Goddess' to wear
a flowering branch
water for lustrations
a special floral garland/necklet for the 'Greenman' to wear
a special floral bouquet to present to the 'Goddess'
a picnic feast, which can be either a sacred meal or a full picnic meal
May Wine or May Juice (see recipes at the end of this ritual)
music for dancing

Days before the Ritual is to take place, gather a work party to create the floral garlands and wreaths that are needed for the performance. You will find full instructions for both, at the end of this ritual.

To begin the ritual, the Priestess and at least two other female attendants approach the area, attended by the maiden who will represent the Goddess for this event. The maiden may be dressed in a very simple robe. The three principals will proceed to cast the circle (raise the temple) in whatever manner is most used by your group. Once this is complete, the attendants will hold a cloth or screen to protect the privacy of the maiden, while the Priestess washes her, having removed the simple robe for the process. When she is washed and dried, and dressed in a simple, floral-printed gown, the screen is put away, and a signal is given to the others, who have awaited nearby, and who will now process, dancing in a serpentine fashion, to the temple, wearing simple floral wreaths and carrying baskets of flowers and garlands to decorate the temple.

Bringing up the rear of the procession is our own version of the 'Greenman', or Jack in the Green, a male decorated with only leaves, and no flowers, carrying the special floral wreath to place upon the head of the 'Goddess'. .

As the procession enters the temple, the bowers or garlands are laid at the outer boundaries of the temple, and the flowers in the baskets are strewn across the temple floor, perfuming the area for the ritual. As the guests deposit their floral tributes, they begin to dance around the temple. Then, when the 'Greenman' crowns the 'Goddess' with a wreath, saying, *"Beautiful is your body and fair this bloom; Accept it from your passionate groom."* He joins the dance which continues only briefly at that point. The 'Greenman' is to be respectful, yet attentive, at this juncture.

When the music stops and while the temple doors are still open, those who have brought their animals may lead them into the temple area, past the 'Goddess', who will lustrate each one with a floral branch dipped in water. (Animal owners may wish to practice this event with their animals ahead of time, to avoid any sudden and untoward reactions to the water droplets.) Words may be spoken at the time of lustration, such as, *"I bless you in the name of the Goddess. May you be fruitful and sound."* After all the animals have been blessed and removed from the temple to a safe holding place, the participants will return to their places in the temple.

Music will begin to play and the 'Greenman' will start the dance, preening and strutting in a suggestive manner, around the 'Goddess', in a courtship manner. He should dance *at least* for the length of a normal musical piece, about 2½ minutes. While he dances, the 'Goddess' watches with interest. When he is finished, he retires to the opposite side of the temple from where the 'Goddess' stands, and she begins her part of the dance. She should dance in a seductive and flirtatious manner, specifically engaging the 'Greenman', and she should also dance *at least* for the same amount of time. Onlookers are encouraged to applaud, make comments and thoroughly enjoy the activity.

When the 'Goddess' has completed her dance, the 'Greenman' joins her in the center of the temple and they dance together, in an straightforwardly suggestive manner. Let this become a bawdy activity for all concerned, dancers and onlookers alike.

At the end of the dancing, a member of the group approaches the couple, offering the 'Goddess' a bouquet of spring flowers, tied with colorful ribbons. The 'Greenman' is offered a floral garland to wear around his neck, made of the same spring flowers, lacking the ribbons. The couple then retires to a corner of the temple to watch the others as they decorate the living tree and cavort joyfully around it.

Each guest is invited to take several ornaments to place upon the tree in as decorative a manner as they can, and when all the decorations have been placed on the tree, music will begin once more, and the company will begin to dance around the May Tree. Be certain that the music you choose is lively and entertaining for all to enjoy. This dance may continue as long as the participants desire it to go on.

When the dancing has finally ended, all will settle upon the flower-strewn temple floor for a picnic feast. The feast may consist only of the sacred meal, if you like, or it can be an actual picnic with a selection of foods. It is suggested that the beverage be May Wine or May Juice, a recipe for which appears at the end of this ritual.

To open the feast, the 'Goddess' announces, *"Now you will eat the rippling fields of wheat, in every bite of bread."*

To which the 'Greenman' will respond, *"Now you will eat the sun that ripened the foods that nourish you."*

And the 'Goddess' will reply, *"Now you will drink the rain that saturated the soil in which it grew."*

And the 'Greenman' continues, *"Now you will know the Earth, from which all blessings flow."*

During the feast, the 'Goddess' and the 'Greenman' are to be seen feeding each other, and others are encouraged to do the same with their chosen partners, or with any others in the temple. The lesson for this sabbat is freedom and fertility, so anything goes, as long as your group is comfortable with that. The feasting may continue as long as the participants are willing to enjoy it, in whatever manner appeals to them, and is acceptable to your group.

At the close of the feast, the 'Goddess' and the 'Greenman' will announce that the ritual is ended. The Priestess and/or Priest, in conjunction with them, open the temple once more, in the manner usually followed by your group.

L'ora d'Estate

Summer Solstice

A fifteen-hour ritual celebration on June 21

Midsummer is a celebration of the Sun, and of divine power. It falls on the longest day of the year, and our ritual will take advantage of the long, sunny day, with a full fourteen hours, from sunrise to sundown, of worship and merriment. It is a festival of coupling, in many forms, not just sexual, although that is a basic form. After this long day, the sun will begin to wane, to be reborn in six months' time, at the Winter Solstice. We will enjoy the sun's power this day and fill ourselves with its joy, to hold in our hearts for the remainder of the year.

The ritual was written for either two genders, or for those who associate themselves with the two genders of deity. Those who are more comfortable with the God figure will play the part of the male in the ritual, while those who are most comfortable with the Goddess figure will play the role of the female. In this way, you might have men dancing as women, or vice versa, and that is how it should be. For each of us has the androgyne within, as the divine is neither all male nor all female, but a bit of both, as the ritual will disclose.

This ritual is a coven call, and will utilize every member of the coven. If you do not have a full coven, perhaps you could work with another coven just for this ritual, to have enough people, or invite guests to join you for the day. I suggest that one person provide the site, which should include privacy, a swimming pool, and enough space to play outdoor games or to do crafts. Of course, there should be a sacred circle. Another person should be responsible for the morning meal, and another for the evening meal. A separate person is to take on the chore of providing the luncheon, which is to be a cook-out or barbecue. Someone must also be responsible to provide beverages for the all-day activities, and water is recommended. There should be music for dancing, or at least a drummer. The season might even bring to mind a flute. Finally, someone should be responsible for games and someone else for crafting and supplies.

Participants will have brought with them to the site a bathing suit as well as robes and playing clothes. Read through the ritual completely before setting your plans, as there are a few surprises, and you wouldn't want to be unprepared.

The Hours

The first hour is Sunrise, when all gather at the site to watch the sun creep up over the horizon and become the brilliant, warm, life-asserting entity we will adore. Singing is suggested, and the song that comes to mind first is the old children's ditty, "You Are My Sunshine". I have posted the lyrics here, for those who may not know them all:

You are my sunshine
My only sunshine
You make me happy
When skies are gray.
You'll never know, dear,
How much I love you.
Please don't take my sunshine away

The other night, dear,
As I lay sleeping
I dreamed I held you in my arms.
When I awoke, dear,
I was mistaken
And I hung my head and I cried.

You are my sunshine,
My only sunshine.
You make me happy
When skies are gray.
You'll never know, dear,
How much I love you.
Please don't take my sunshine away.

Fill the hour with other sunny songs and little dances to welcome the sun this day.

The second hour is for your body. Having calmly sung and danced to the sunrise, you are now sufficiently warmed-up, and can begin exercising. If one of your members is adept at exercising, perhaps s/he could lead the activity. Just be certain to take it easy for those members who may not be used to such a work out, allowing them to work at their own pace, and rest when they feel the need. Also be sure to allow at least a fifteen-minute cool-down time as the hour ends.

The third hour is for nourishment. Time for breakfast. Serve food that is simple, easy to prepare and hearty for the body. Foods that are usually a part of any Midsummer celebration could include:

The fourth hour is for meditation. The members are permitted a 20-minute personal meditation time, followed by a 20-minute guided meditation. Those who do not care to take part in the first part of this activity can simply rest quietly while the others meditate. Following is the script for the guided meditation:

The fifth and sixth hours are active. Games can be set up and played. Anything from volleyball to croquet can be enjoyed in the sun, and run the gamut from very active to only mildly active. For those who cannot partake of sport, set up a crafting area where members can create sun symbols, like the Ojo de Dios, a solar wheel, a sun face with emanating rays, or even a lion's mane (if someone works well with yarn) to wear in the dancing later in the day.

The seventh, eighth and ninth hours are wet and wild. Time to strip down to a bathing costume and enjoy the water, sparkling with the sun's light dancing on its surface. Sometime during these hours, the person in charge of luncheon should set up the cookfire and begin to prepare the groceries that will feed the coven a midday meal. Be sure that everyone has enough to eat, and that they are protected from any harmful rays of the sun. He is stronger than we, and doesn't always know His own strength.

The tenth hour is for the Nines. Each of nine members of the group, in a circle with all the members, will, in turn, leave the outer circle and walk within it, deosil, slowly and thoughtfully, three times. S'He will come to the center of the circle and will choose a note from a basket which is placed on the altar there, and read it aloud. The reading should be slow enough to be understood, and clearly spoken, and loud enough that everyone can hear it. Once read, the note is to be dropped into an empty basket, where all the notes will be collected for burning. Following is suggested text for the Nines:

"Deity is not a nameless male, who bullies us into following his rules for our growth, with threats of eternal punishment."

"Deity is both male and female, and is loving and understanding."

"Deity is creative and peaceful; it gives life and protects it."

"Deity awaits our wakening – our remembrance – our reconstruction of the old ways, patiently, lovingly."

"Deity accepts the sacrifice of our prayers, and our tears, and our laughter."

"Deity encourages joy and consoles sorrow."

"Deity calls us to worship, but does not demand it of us."

"Deity delights in us, for we are the beloved children; we are the product of divine love."

"Deity dwells within us, each and every one; empowering our every thought."

Following the Nines, the person acting as Priestess and the person acting as Priest enter the center of the circle. The Priestess walks slowly around the circle, widdershins, in a mildly flirtatious manner, while the Priest watches from the center. She strolls three times around, then approaches him, saying,

"I am a gentle, peaceable doe, roaming the forest – beloved of the Goddess."

The Priest now circles around while the Priestess watches, but he travels deosil, three times, as well. When completed, he approached her, saying,

"I am the fierce, horned stag, standing by you – ready to protect you from all harm."

Music plays and they each continue their own circuit, in their own directions, three times around, and return to the center. This part of the dance can be an acting-out of the sentiment just spoken, if they wish.

She now travels deosil three times, slowly again, and approaching him, says,

"I am a delicate blossom, bursting with color and scent."

He travels three times widdershins around and comes to her in the center, saying,

"I am a powerful tree, watching over you, strong and capable."

They travel in their own directions, again, not together, three times, slowly to the music.

This time, after traveling widdershins, the priestess says,

"I am the silver moonlight, the very starshine."

The priest, having traveled deosil, says,

"I am the golden sunlight, the very dayshine."

They dance in opposite directions, once more, to the music.

Again they change directions, and she declares,

"I am a word; I am poetry and information. I sing the Goddess."

He declares,

"I am a spear; I am loyalty and protection. I radiate the God."

They dance in opposite directions.

Switching directions again, she states,

"I am a witch, an enchanter."

He says,

"I am a wizard, a charmer."

This time they dance together in the same direction, for they are two halves of the same divine entity.

Should this activity intrude upon the activity for the following hour, no harm is intended. It is important that the Priest and Priestess complete their dance and that the participants understand the play. If it has cut into the time allotted for the eleventh hour, simply shorten the eleventh hour by the same amount of time.

The eleventh hour is for problem solving. A stately procession, with only a drum playing softly, meanders across and through a labyrinth, processing in and out again, in silence. Each member can use the time to ponder her or his difficulties and seek answers from the divine source within.

The twelfth hour is for the Thirteen Prayers. These are 13 praying people, who can be volunteers at the last possible moment, so that they aren't fully aware of what they will be asked to say. Their words must come from the immediate heart, and not something practiced and memorized. One member stands in the center of the circle, with a basket of small notes, to distribute to the volunteers. The notes are suggestions for prayers to be created by the volunteer, for the good of all the members of the coven. In other words, these prayers are not "*I*" prayers, they are "*We*" prayers.

Following are suggestions for the notes' texts:

Seek the spirit within, commune with the divine

Pray in spite of problems

See opportunities for growth in the challenges that attack us

Acknowledge our own transgressions, and be compassionate and forgiving

Develop a healing touch, not just for illness

Dedicate ourselves in spirit through our responsibilities

Give gratitude for blessings

Show companionship and support for each other

Share unselfishly

Be patient with the divine

Offer hope and comfort to others in need

Be a divine light to others through your own life

Rejoice in the god or goddess

The thirteenth hour is for the dance. Loosen up your muscles and dance with abandon. Work up an appetite, raise power.

The fourteenth hour is for Dinner. This could be something pre-arranged and simply re-heated, or it could be cooked during this hour, provided there remains enough time for each person to eat his or her fill. All remnants of Dinner should be cleared away before the fifteenth hour begins.

The fifteenth and final hour is Sunset. Once again, the singing or playing of Sun songs should be the activity. A lovely, quiet song for sunset is "*Sunshine on my Shoulders*". The lyrics, written by John Denver, Dick Kniss and Mike Taylor are reproduced here:

"Sunshine on my shoulders makes me happy

Sunshine in my eyes can make me cry
Sunshine on the water looks so lovely
Sunshine almost always makes me high

If I had a day that I could give you
I'd give to you a day just like today
If I had a song that I could sing for you
I'd sing a song to make you feel this way

Sunshine on my shoulders makes me happy
Sunshine in my eyes can make me cry
Sunshine on the water looks so lovely
Sunshine almost always makes me high

If I had a tale that I could tell you
I'd tell a tale sure to make you smile
If I had a wish that I could wish for you
I'd make a wish for sunshine all the while

Sunshine on my shoulders makes me happy
Sunshine in my eyes can make me cry
Sunshine on the water looks so lovely
Sunshine almost always makes me high
Sunshine almost all the time makes me high"

Summerfest

A Fairy Ritual

It is suggested, since there is so much to say, that you write the short speeches on leaf-shaped pieces of paper from which you may read in the circle. The altar should be set as usual, with cake and wine and a chalice, with fairy wine and warmed milk, with real butter pats and tiny bits of cake and very small chalices, cups and plates*, two baskets (one with foil-wrapped chocolate coins), a bowl of water and a floating candle, a beeswax candle and a cauldron in which a fire can be made.

Each guest has been told beforehand to bring a shiny object or two for the fae, some small bits of colored ribbons, and a small paper upon which they have written of a harm that needs be banished.

* Small chalices, cups and plates can be found in stores that sell doll or dollhouse furnishings.

The outer confines of the circle should be sprinkled generously with salt. I suggest using blessed kosher salt, since it's not pulverized so small you can't see it on the ground. On top of the salt, you should sprinkle flowers, since this is a Midsummer ritual, and the flowers are readily available. Intone your traditional greeting to the elements and guests, light the incense (if you're using it) and take the center of the circle.

"I come before you to join with the powers of nature and to celebrate with the fae. I invite all the fae folk of good intent to join us here, for on this night the veil between the world of humans and the world of the fae is thin. We can see and hear you and you can see and hear us. Together let us celebrate Midsummer Magic."

Facing the north,

"Spirits of the forests and meadows, come along to play with us, bringing your best behavior, and there will be fairy wine." Pour the fairy wine into small chalices.

Facing the west,

"Denizens of the deep, merfolk and nymphs, come along to play, bringing your best behavior, and there will be butter." Place pats of real butter onto small plates.

Facing the south,

"Sunbeams of delight, fireflies and dwellers in the flames, come along to play, bringing your best behavior, and there will be warm milk." Pour warmed milk into small cups.

Facing the east,

"Flitting fairies, butterflies and spirits of the moon, come along to play, bringing your best behavior, and there will be

cake."

Place bits of sweet cake on small plates.

"Accept these offerings as tokens of our love for you, and our willingness to learn from you."

Light a flame in the cauldron.

"Here we banish all that has harmed us in the past year, by the powers of earth, air, water and fire. May we know that power by the ground beneath our feet, the wind in our hair, the tears of joy we shed and the passion in our spirits."

Each guest is invited to approach the flame to drop in a small paper that names the harm that is to be banished from her or his life.

Collect bits of colored ribbon from all the guests into a small basket for the fairies. When this is done, collect small shiny objects, along with chocolate coins, in another basket for them. Place these baskets on either side of the altar,

"Come beloved fae folk, children of the hidden realm. Accept these gifts as your own. Lend us your mystical power to preserve the natural potency of the earth."

Join hands with all the guests in the circle, inviting the fae to dance with you. The dance must begin in a deosil (clockwise) direction, but from time to time, should change direction, and grow a bit faster with each change. The dance will continue until you can no longer continue. When releasing the power you've raised, send it forth to the fae, to use as they see fit to heal the earth and the universe.

Light a beeswax candle,

"Here burns the earth and the air."

Light a floating candle in a bowl of water,

"Here burns a flame in the water."

"As the elements are joined by burning, so let the humans and the fae be joined by the passion in our hearts."

Cut the cake or bread for the sacred meal and pour the wine into the chalice.

"May this cake (bread) be the very essence of the Goddess, and may our fairy friends partake of Her blessing."

Distribute the cake, saying, *"May you never hunger."*

"May this wine be the very essence of the God, and may our fairy friends partake of His blessing."

Pass the chalice, saying, *"May you never thirst."*

Dismiss the fairy folk

Facing the north,

"Spirits of the forests and meadows, thank you for playing with us and we will welcome you again soon. You may now return to your own realm."

Facing the west,

"Denizens of the deep, merfolk and nymphs, thank you for playing with us and we will welcome you again soon. You may now return to your own realm."

Facing the south,

"Sunbeams of delight, fireflies and dwellers in the flames, thank you for playing with us and we will welcome you again soon. You may now return to your own realm."

Facing the east,

"Flitting fairies, butterflies and spirits of the moon, thank you for playing with us and we will welcome you again soon. You may now return to your own realm."

Dismiss the elements and thank the gods for their protection. Open the circle.

La Giornata della Dea

Goddess Day

The month of August is filled with days that are sacred to one Great Mother Goddess or another. You alone may determine which Goddess and which day you will choose to honor for this festival.

As suggestions, let me offer:

August 2 is sacred to the Black Madonna and to Habondia
August 3 is sacred to the Greek Goddess Artemis
August 12 is sacred to the Lights of Isis
August 13 is sacred to the Roman Goddess Diana
August 15 is sacred to Cybele, the Great Mother, as well as to Vesta, Goddess of the Hearth
August 17 is sacred to the Roman Goddess Diana
August 20 is sacred to the Sumerian Goddess Innana

In 1945, in a cave, texts were discovered from the Nag Hammadi Library, in which are numerous references to the Great Mother in writings that were deliberately excluded from the established version of the Bible. For instance, the *Trimorphic Protennoia* (Triple-formed Primal Thought) begins with a divine personage stating: *"I am the Thought that dwells in the Light, She who exists before the All, I move in every creature, I am the invisible One within the All."*

The Apocryphon of John offers a description of the Great Mother, from the invisible Spirit: *"She became the womb of everything, for it is She who is prior to them all, the Mother-Father, the first man, the holy Spirit, the thrice-male, the thrice-powerful, the thrice-named androgynous One, and the eternal aeon among the invisible Ones, and the first to come forth."* Later, in the same work, the Great Mother Trinity speaks to John: *"I am the one who is with you always. I am the Father; I am the Mother; I am the Son."* It is interesting that the text uses the Hebrew word *ruah* instead of the Greek *pneuma* for Spirit. *Pneuma* is a masculine word, while *ruah* is feminine.

With this in mind, you are certainly performing an ancient practice of respect for the Great Mother, whether you indulge in this particular ritual or one of your own making.

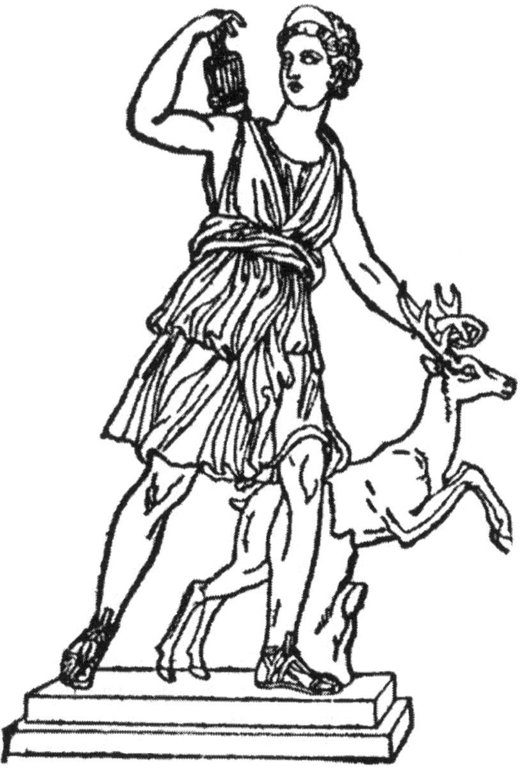

This ritual requires:
a cauldron filled at least halfway with water
a collection of small pebbles or stones
candles to represent both the Goddess and the God
a small offering of something that has value to each guest (more about this in a moment)
incense
a flower for each participant, in a container at the altar
a woman who will represent the Goddess in the flesh and seven garments or artifacts to clothe the "Goddess" with her attributes
lustrating water and a towel

You will also need:
a blessed beverage and a chalice from which to drink it
an inner temple of Darkness (see the suggested method, below)
a Goddess chest in which are placed objects that require a person to undergo a speech or an activity
an empty basket to receive those objects once the chore has been completed
'Cakes and Ale' for the sacred meal

Each guest will have been told in advance to bring an offering for a local food pantry. This should be a food that will not spoil if it must wait to be dispersed, and if in a can, should be far enough from the expiration date to permit such a wait. If there is a member of the ritual group who is presently undergoing particular hard times, the food may be donated to that member, instead of to a food pantry, if the group agrees.

To begin the ritual, the woman who will represent the Goddess, along with the Priestess and at least two attendants go alone to the sacred area, and they cast the circle, or, more correctly, raise the temple. During this process, the elements are called, the Goddess and God candles are lit and the deities are invited to attend.

The Priestess and attendants then 'bathe' the Goddess' representative, lustrating her head and hands, and offer a towel to dry her. Once this has been accomplished, a signal is given to the other participants, who have been waiting a short distance away for this moment. They begin a slow, somber procession to the temple, carrying the seven garments and artifacts that will clothe the "Goddess". (A cloak, if offered, should be the last item delivered, and should be carried by the Priest.)

If the Goddess substitute is agreeable, and the remainder of your group is comfortable with it (and if the weather cooperates), she may stand in the center of the temple, nude, awaiting her garments. Failing that, she might wear a simple undergown, but no ornament or jewelry of any kind. The Priestess and attendants should stand close by her, as they will assist her in donning the garments as they arrive. As a piece arrives, the carrier can, if you wish, identify what is carried, what it signifies and which Goddess you have chosen to honor with this gift.

Suggestions for the garments and artifacts, the attributes that accompany them, and the Goddesses of those attributes, follow:

Veil - Goddess of Justice (Astrea, Dike, Justitia, Maat, Portia, Themis)
Tiara or Crown with stars - Queen of the Heavens (Anat, Asherah, Astarte, Hera, Innana, Isis, Juno)
Necklace - Goddess of Beauty (Erzulie, Freya, Hathor, Hebe, Hora, Zoria)
Ring - Great Mother (Cybele, Devi, Dindymene, Ops)
Girdle - Protector of the Children (Bast, Caireen, Demeter, Maia, Persephone)
Staff - Goddess of Wisdom (Athene, Minerva, Neith, Saraswati, Sophia)
Garter - Goddess of Love and Sexuality (Aine, Anahita, Aphrodite, Venus, Voluptas)
Cloak - Mother of the Gods (Gaea, Ishtar, Rhea, Shakti)

This list (or any other attributes and garments you choose) can be used in a manner, such as:

"Receive this veil, which is the symbol of Your unbiased Justice."

"Wear this crown, which demonstrates Your power over the heavens."

"This necklace represents Your eternal beauty."

"This ring is a symbol of Your divine Motherhood."

"With this girdle we recognize that You protect all the children."

"The staff stands for Your great wisdom."

"The garter symbolizes Your sexuality."

"This cloak envelops the Mother of all the Gods."

Once the "Goddess" is fully clothed, she will lead all the others in a procession three times around the inside of the temple, before she is seated on a decorated 'throne' for the remainder of most of the proceedings. The procession need not be a somber one, but joyful, in that the Goddess has been ritually honored on earth once more.

A table is placed before the 'Goddess', upon which is the cauldron of water and the pebbles. Each participant, in turn, approaches the table, and, taking one pebble for each name, identifies the female ancestor who has touched her or his spirit in some significant way. A single sentence will suffice to identify these honored females, such as: *"This is for Mabel, my mother, who suffered the grief of leaving her first children behind, beginning a new family, elsewhere. This is for Elisa, my grandmother, who brought the faith of the old country here to me."* Each guest is invited to name as many females (and pebbles) in this manner as s/he wishes. As a name is mentioned, a pebble is dropped into the cauldron of water.

When the guests have identified all the females desired, a moment of meditative silence prevails, during which soft music may be played, while the participants prepare for the next offering. Incense is lighted and wafted over the entire temple.

Each guest then approaches the "Goddess" and makes her or his offering, placing the food product in a basket or box that has been placed beside her.

The Darkness is now erected within the temple, in that dark-colored fabric is attached to stakes or lines in such a way as to permit passage within the fabric while circumventing the temple. Within The Darkness, you might wish to display 'visions' of the Underworld, Death, Grieving, etc. Here is a suggested manner of creating The Darkness, drawn by Julie Durocher, whose website is:

www.durochers.org/journalarchives/2004_05_01_archive.html:

Each participant, in turn, must travel through The Darkness, in absolute silence, wearing only an inner garment, or in the nude, if the group and the guest are agreeable. This is a purification exercise, and should affect each participant in some personal way.

Exiting The Darkness, the guest is permitted to don her or his garment once more, and to partake of a blessed beverage. I suggest Barley Water, a recipe for which can be found at the end of this ritual. The beverage is to be set upon a table at the exit of The Darkness, and should be offered personally by the 'Goddess'..

When each participant has completed the Journey through Darkness (with the exception of the 'Goddess'), and taken the blessed beverage, each will approach the seated 'Goddess' once more, this time taking a blossom, which is in a container near the cauldron that now contains pebbles in the water, and places the blossom on the water, while stating the reasons s/he honors her or him self, and the feminine energy within.

Each guest is then invited to remove one object from the 'Goddess'' chest, which is situated beside her 'throne'. The objects are to be symbolic of various life journeys, like an egg to symbolize birth, seeds to symbolize growth, a diploma to symbolize wisdom, etc. Each symbol should be clear enough to permit the chooser to know immediately what chore is required. S/he may decide to enact an activity related to that symbol, or to speak about her or his experience in that relationship - briefly, and so on. The chores are to be performed after all participants have drawn from the chest. As a chore is completed, the performer may deposit the symbol in the empty basket provided for that purpose.

Immediately after the conclusion of all chores, you may begin the sacred meal, to ground and refresh all the participants. The blessed feast will serve to invigorate them after the solemn activities just completed.

Music may then be played once more, this time more playful and entertaining strains, and the guests may choose to dance about the 'Goddess', who will be invited to join them in the Dance of Joy. The dancing should continue until no one is willing to dance longer, and all are seated on the earth (or, in the case of the 'Goddess', on her 'throne').

At this point, the Priestess and Priest release the elements, thank the deities that were invited to witness, open the temple, and dismiss the participants.

Abbondanza!

Abundance!

A Fall Equinox Ritual

This is unlike any other ritual, in that no circle is cast, and it isn't held on sacred ground or in a secluded space. This is, in fact, a Witch's Thanksgiving.

For this ritual, you will need a table large enough to hold the feast and seat all those you have invited to be a part of your Thanksgiving Feast. You will also need chairs for each of those invited.

At each place setting, you will have put either a bulb or a seedling, ready for planting, along with a slip of paper and a writing implement. There should also be an unlit votive candle at each place.

Away from the eating table, you will have set up a small table/altar holding a candle taper, a small amount of the dried herb Rue, and a dish or pot in which little fires can be lit safely. All of this should be displayed around a statue or picture of the Goddess and God. Be sure to have a trivet under the burning dish to keep the heat away from the table top, and have matches handy to light the fires and candles.

All the food that is to be served at your Thanksgiving Feast is to be locally grown. That is, if it didn't grow in the geographical area where you are eating it, it shouldn't be on your table. This goes for all fruits and vegetables, beverages, meats and desserts. I realize that this rather limits your usual choices, but if you do a little research, you can still manage to put together a wondrous feast, using only items purchased at local farmer's markets, neighborhood farms, etc. Some of the foods can have been canned (preserved), but they must have been locally-grown before the processing.

When all the food is ready for consumption, and the table is set, you may call your guests to the table. They must all stand behind their chairs for the beginning ceremony. The eldest female is to be seated at the head of the table, and the eldest male opposite her at the other head of the table. All other guests remain standing, holding hands, behind their chairs. (You might have put place cards at each plate, so there will be no confusion at this juncture.)

Beginning at the left of the eldest female, who is seated, each guest will take a turn to state their gratitude for the season. They may speak of their personal and spiritual harvest, or of mundane matters that have been successful for them through this past season, or whatever they most feel grateful for at this time, or things they learned over the year.

Since this is a time of balance and harvest, we must honor both the negative and the positive, noting the sweetness of the harvest as well as the bitter harvests that some may bear. Each guest may bring up the failures and negative aspects of the past year, but must finish their remarks with the more positive observations.

Each should be given enough time to complete their thoughts, although they should be aware that there are many others waiting their turn to speak. When the turn comes around to the seated eldest male, he may speak from his seated position, and the turn passes to his left on around the table. As it comes to the seated female, she remains seated and gives not only her own thoughts, but a general blessing for the feast and the company with which to share it. She might say something like, *"As this food nourishes us all, May it teach us to nourish each other."*

We've also used, *"Bless the earth who gives us our food. Bless the sun who makes it so good. Bless the people who farmed the earth, to give us everything here of worth."*

Then and only then, all may be seated and the feast may begin!

It is hoped that there will be stimulating conversation at the table while feasting, which is entertaining and amusing for all concerned.

After the feast has come to an end, each guest is asked to write on their slip of paper something they wish to release from their consciousness this season. It could be things that did not go well for them this year, negative feelings, regrets, failures, disappointments, etc. This should not be discussed openly, but simply written on the paper.

When this is done, each person should take their paper and their still-unlit votive candle to the burning altar or table. There, the candle taper should be lit, and a tiny pinch of rue should be placed upon paper, which is then either folded to enclose the herb, or twisted closed around it. The paper is set aflame with a match, not from the candle flame, and set into the burning pot. Concentrate upon the things written on the paper being removed as the paper burns. When the guest feels that the negativity has been sent to the Gods, s/he may then light the votive candle, and leave it in front of the statue or picture representation there.

Having rid themselves of their regrets, the guests can now collect the bulb or plant that was at their place at the table, and remove to a planting area. This can be outside, or, if the weather isn't cooperating, to a place where flower pots are waiting with earth for planting, along with hand spades for the purpose. The seedlings should be transplanted into larger pots, or into the ground, and the bulbs should be potted or planted in the soil outside. As the planting or transplanting is being accomplished, the guest should concentrate upon expected joys and successes for the coming year, infusing those thoughts into the plant or bulb. As the plant grows, so does the success of those ventures, hopes and ideas.

il Viaggio delle Morte

Journey of Death

This ritual is held on October 31.

This ritual requires quite a bit of preparation. Be sure to read the entire ritual, making notes as you go along, so as to include all the different aspects of the journey into your own ritual. However, should any aspect here presented be inappropriate for your group, leave it out, or substitute something more befitting.

You will lay out a serpentine pathway, perhaps in a wooded area, but at least in an area that will be very dark when the sun sets. You might use white stones to outline the pathway for your guests, or even some stones that glow in the dark.

Set up each area of visitation beforehand, in such a way as to represent the spirit of the lesson. The altars you must consider are:
(1) a table littered with unlit candles, and one lit candle;
(2) a table with bones (if you can get them) and photographs of ancestors (yours, your guests', or any you find that will suffice), slips of paper and writing instruments, garden spades and soft earth for burying small mementoes brought along by the guests;
(3) a table scattered with herbs next to a burning cauldron;
(4) a table scattered with large seeds and nuts, and
(5) a selection of very small mirrors to be scattered on the ground (this area must be clear overhead to allow the moon to be visible).

Narrative

It is a chill October evening; the sky is a deep, dark hue, the moon is a crone in dark robes, and the stars are brilliant, smiling at the Mother in her harvest glory.

The veil between light and dark
between visible and invisible
between living and dead
is thinnest now.

Now we can see in the dark.

We can enter another reality, and dwell for a time with the crone.

Welcome.

Before you is a table, strewn with candles. One candle is alight. Take up a candle and light it from the source. Once lit, follow me onto the dark pathway.

Trust your inner guidance. Let us find what the Goddess and God have left for us.

(Travel to the next altar)

Behold the altar of mourning, filled with the bones of ancestors, photographs of loved ones when they were with us. Remember them, but do not grieve longer. They have gone on to a new life: a life of joy and discovery. A headstone centers the altar, inviting us to let go of that which holds us to the pain. Death is here in the darkness.

Ancestors, loved ones, all those who came before and those who have passed over into their own next world, are here. Those who suffered horribly at the hands of good men and women, simply because they were different, are here.

A feast is spread here for them, to nourish their journey into forevermore.

Take but a moment to greet your forebears. You may leave a gift or a memento, if you have brought one with you. Take a slip of paper, offered here, and record what holds you from joy in your own, heart-felt words. Hold the paper until we reach the altar of morning, where all will be lifted from you.

A small spade is here for you to dig into the loose earth, making a hole to hold your gifts, and your thoughts of your loved ones. Bury them in the Mother, where the ancestors will receive them.

Let us move on from here.

(Travel to the next altar)

Behold the altar of morning, festooned with herbs for banishing. Let the paper of your words hold a pinch of these herbs, as you consider leaving this pain behind you. Fold the paper three times. Place the paper and herb on the pyre that burns here, awaiting your need. Watch your pain burn away, determining that you will be rid of it from your life. When the last trace of the paper has burned, give it not one more thought, for thought gives truth, and on the page that burns is an untruth. Give it not new life. Leave it behind and move on with me.

(Travel to the next altar)

Behold the altar of today
scattered with seeds
burgeoning with life
awaiting you
needing you.

Take as many seeds as you can name for the positive changes you wish to see in your life in this new year. What will you plan in your fertile mind to bear affirmative fruit within you? Beseech the Goddess and God who watch over the seeds to activate the seeds you have named, as you consume the seeds, making their magic a part of your own.

Nourished, move along with me.

(Travel to the next altar)

Behold the altar of tomorrow, where nothing is known, and everything is familiar.

No table stands before you.
No Goddess, no God.
No candles burn.
No incense smolders.

But, something shiny on the earth before you beckons you. Pick it up – hold it. Catch the edge of the moon in its surface. Look to see what it tells you there. Feel the words enter your consciousness. Carry the mirror and the message with you as you move along with me.

(Travel to the next area)

We come now to where we began, to the here and now, to the space within the enveloping circle. Welcome home. Remember your harvest journey. Be Blessed.

Shadowfest

Feast of the Ancestors

This is a shorter, more traditional Shadowfest ritual, which may suit your purposes more often than the *Viaggio di Morte*. It is also one that is to be accomplished by a solitary practitioner.

You will need to have an altar set up, facing the west, with wine, cake, a red candle, an apple (and a knife to cut it).

"I call to my ancestors, all those who came before me and those of whom I am a part. Your breath is my breath. Your voice is in my throat. Your song is in my ear.

"My Goddess, you have left me, to live and love and become the Lady of Darkness. Now you will rest and await the Child of Tomorrow, the seed who will restore light unto me. All that was once green and lush, fruitful and fertile, is now withered and faded, for the Earth grows cold without you. But I sorrow not, for I know that you will return. I stand unafraid and I embrace the darkness that lays before me. You will protect me, and Your great wisdom will guide me. I am blessed by the Darkness.

"I offer this apple in remembrance of my ancestors and their love for you. Apples are a symbol of the dead, and within them is the symbol of life."

Cut the apple in half horizontally, to expose the pentagram within. Eat only from one half of the apple, leaving the other half for the spirits.

"I light this candle to illuminate the path for my ancestors to travel through the veil to me, to visit me with their understanding"
Light the red candle.

"May the God bless this wine, as He comes to guard me through the Darkness."

Hold the wine aloft for a moment, and then drink.

"May the Goddess bless this cake, as She retires for a time, before Her triumphal return."

Hold the cake aloft for a moment, and then eat.

"The wheel has turned, but I do not sorrow. For I dwell in the womb of the Goddess of the Night, who comforts me with every breath I take.

"My beloved ancestors, you may return to the Summerland where you await your rebirth. Thank you for your wisdom and your kindness.

"My Goddess and my God, you have blessed me once more with Your presence and your guidance. Thank you for your wisdom and your kindness to me.

I release the circle now, and return to my mundane world. So mote it be."

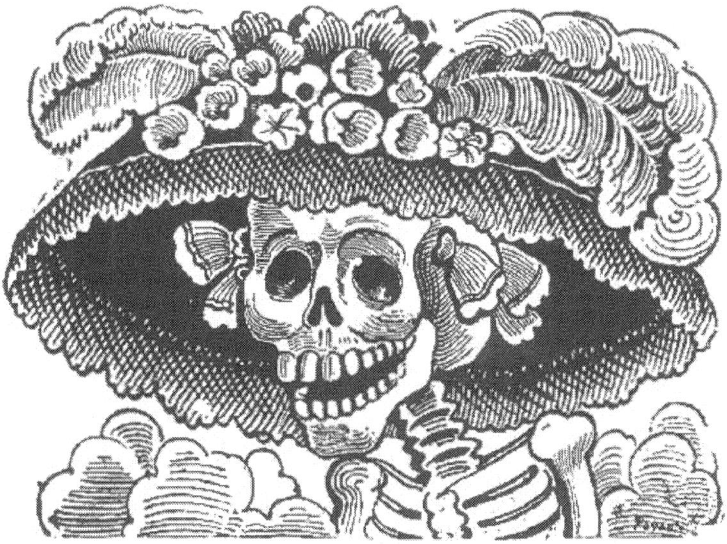

Rites of Passage

Rites of Passage are ritual events that mark a person's progress from one position to another. These are often ceremonies surrounding things like puberty, coming of age, marriage and death, as well as baptism, initiation, dedication, etc. A broad definition of a rite of passage can be a ritual that marks a change in a person's social or sexual status; a mile post or landmark in one's life; a life changing experience; or even a transition between an individual's life stages. These rites are ceremonies to celebrate the natural transitions that we humans all experience.

Honoring the important milestones of human development with ritual helps us to stay in touch with our own natural cycles. Rites of passage generally affirm community solidarity.

Previously, rituals like Baptisms, in which the baby would be exorcized of all previous sin, anointed and blessed as received into the house of the deity; Confirmations, when the bishop would lay hands upon the child, to strengthen it against any assault by demons, and give the child an additional 'sainted' name to signify that strength; Marriage, in which the church formally recognized the union of a man and woman to cohabit; and Churching, when the mother of a newly-born child was purified after the ordeal of childbirth; prevailed. The Reformists objected to each of these rituals, among others, because they appeared to contain elements of 'magic' in them, and, in the case of Churching, because it presumed that childbirth was something dirty that needed to be cleansed (or forgiven) before the woman was considered worthy once more.

We in the goddess community prefer to think of the rites of passage as times for celebration, and for remembrance of the Goddess' love for Her children.

A rite of passage can mean many things for different people. They vary among cultures and also among ages of the participants. Some passages can require rather intense preparation of the person who is progressing to a new life stage, and some simply seem to slip past us.

Dedication Ritual

This is a ritual I designed to permit several young witches to self-dedicate at the same time, together. It was a wonderful experience, as each of us brought our own energy into the ritual, and shared it with our new-found sisters. The ritual was originally written for women only, but it can be altered to accommodate men if they are part of your group. I do not mention a priest or priestess here because all participants are being dedicated, therefore, the 'leader' is simply the hostess or host. Also please note that although only the Goddess is called upon in this circle, your tradition may alter the wording to include the God as well, not only in the charging but also in the blessings.

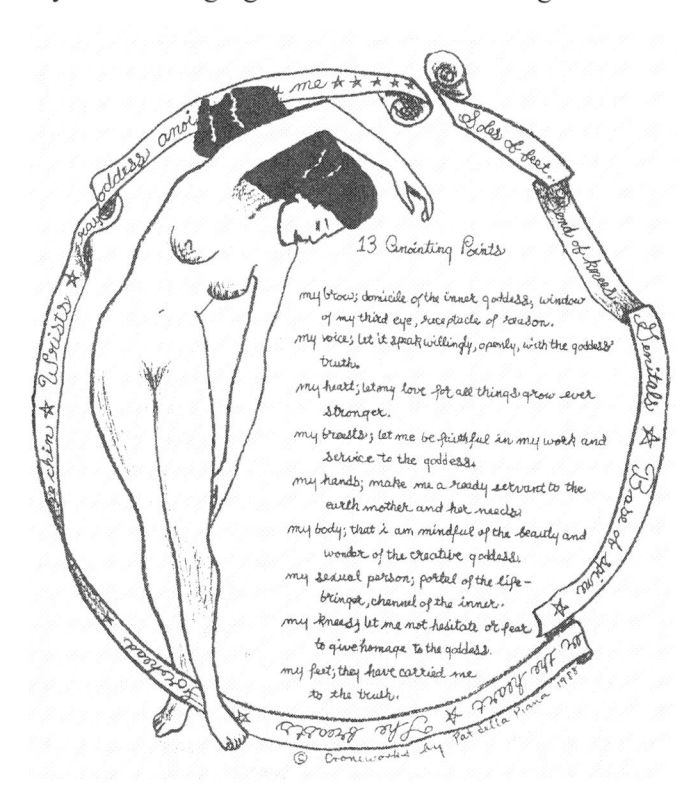

13 Anointing Points

my brow; domicile of the inner goddess, window of my third eye, receptacle of reason.
my voice; let it speak willingly, openly, with the goddess' truth.
my heart; let my love for all things grow ever stronger.
my breasts; let me be faithful in my work and service to the goddess.
my hands; make me a ready servant to the earth mother and her needs.
my body; that I am mindful of the beauty and wonder of the creative goddess.
my sexual person; portal of the life-bringer, channel of the inner.
my knees; let me not hesitate or fear to give homage to the goddess.
my feet; they have carried me to the truth.

First, purify the circle area with salt and water, saying: *A Blessing on all those who are called to this circle."*

Light the altar candle. On the altar are a cauldron with charcoal burning, herbs to add to the cauldron, a bell, a red ritual candle [additional red votive candles if needed, for people who come without one], cakes, wine, and a fire source, like the sacred Bic. Each person is to have brought with them a personal red candle, usually of votive size.

In front of each dedicant is a small table which will act as her altar for the purpose of this ritual. She may decorate her altar as she determines is effective for her, but this should not take more than one or two minutes of time.

Welcome the celebrants. As each person enters, the host/ess blesses them in the configuration of a pentagram with pure spring water, saying:

"Be born of water (right shoulder),
Cleansing (left shoulder),
Powerful (right hip),
Flowing (third eye),
Healing (left hip),
You are goddess (right shoulder)."

Kiss the person's cheek and allow them entrance into the circle, saying:

"You are beloved of the goddess; welcome to Her altar.□

Cast the circle with an athame.

At the East, light the incense. □*The scent of dedication inspires us. You who are breath, radiate your light to us.*□

At the South, light the red candles. *"The flame of candles impassions us. You who are heart, burn your flame in us."*

At the West, dip a finger in a bowl of water to make waves. *"The ripples of water help us understand. You who are blood, flow through us."*

At the North, open the dish of salt, touching it. *"The salt of earth enhances our reason You who are body, fortify us."*

Return to the center and address above the circle *"You who are spirit, empower us. So Mote It Be."*

"As above, So below; As without, So within; As the Universe, So the Circle, So Mote It Be."

Invoke the goddess:

"Mother, wrap your cloak around us, and we will be protected. Encircle us with love and we will be protected. Share yourself with us tonight and we will be protected. Here we stand, between the worlds, safe from harm. We ask You to attend our circle that we may honor You. Come forth, Goddess, and be one with us! So Mote it Be!"
Charge the coven:

"Welcome, to our circle. We are here to name and dedicate ourselves to Goddess and to each other. I charge you all, cleanse your hearts and minds, that only truth be spoken, and only truth be heard.

Light white candles.

Begin by saying your first name, the relationship and name of someone who was important to you in your past, and the way you express your worship.

For instance: *"I am Patricia, granddaughter of Elisa. I am a witch."*

When all have completed their introductions, ring the bell three times.

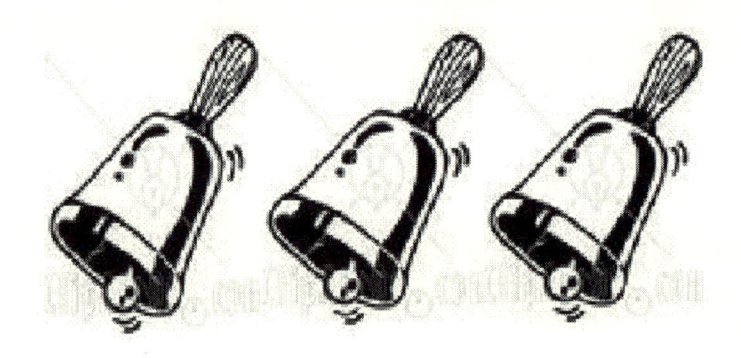

Host/ess lights own votive red candle from the ritual candle.

"Please light your own candle, in turn, and speak your dedication to the Goddess, in your own words. If you have a magical name you choose to be known by, use it now."

"I, ____ , dedicate myself to serve the Goddess in whatever way She requires of me. I feel Her heartbeat in my breast."

Each dedicant will use her own words, which she may read if necessary, as, going deosil around the circle, lights a candle and speaks her personal dedication.

The following is a 'quick' version of the blessing. If you have enough time and space, the host/ess should perform the blessing upon each participant. When the ritual was first used, the circle experience of the participants was unknown to the priestess and she requested that they simply imitate her, leading their own blessing.

Host/ess: *"Let us be blessed by Goddess... Repeat after me."*

Touch (or kiss) top of head *"Bless us. We are Your children"*

Touch (or kiss) third eye *"Bless our sight to see the path before us"*

Touch (or kiss) lips *"Bless our mouths to speak Your name with honor"*

Touch (or kiss) heart *"Bless our hearts to be open to You and to our sisters and brothers"*

Touch (or kiss) abdomen *"Bless our bodies to be filled with energy to live our lives"*

Touch (or kiss) lower belly *"Bless our emotions, for all acts of love and pleasure are Your rituals"*

Touch (or kiss) legs *"Bless our legs to walk in Your paths as our selves"*

Touch (or kiss) hands together *"Bless our hands to do Your work together with our sisters and brothers"*

Touch (or kiss) head again *"Bless us. We are part of You. We are Goddess. So Mote it Be."*

Ring the bell three times.

Hold the plate of cakes.

"Goddess, we ask you to fill this food with the power of life, that we may partake of the wisdom of the ages; we will see the ancient ways more clearly and understand fully. So Mote it Be."

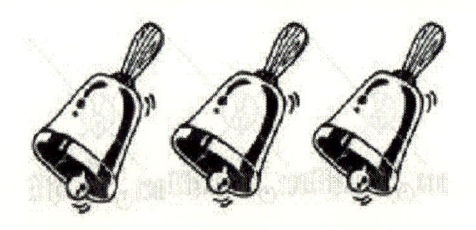

Crumble a bit of food on the earth for tribute, then pass the plate, saying,

"May you never hunger."

Hold the chalice of wine.

"Goddess, we ask you to fill this wine with the force of nature, that we will share in the power of time, of fire, and rain, and things that are wild and free, as we are meant to be. So Mote it Be."

Spill a bit of beverage on the earth for tribute, then, pass the chalice, saying,

"May you never thirst."

When all have partaken, ring the bell three times.

Thank the gods:

"We thank You, Goddess, for being here with us to witness our dedication to You and to feast with us. Now may all beings and elementals who have been attracted to our circle be on their way, harming none. We have been enriched by your presence. Go if you must to your own realms, with our thanks. Blessed Be.

Mother, your love has protected us; again we thank you. We have finished our work. Stay within your circle if you wish."

To the participants:

"The circle is open, but unbroken.

May the love of the Goddess be ever in your hearts.

Merry meet, merry part and merry meet again.

Blessed Be! Blessed Be! Blessed Be!"

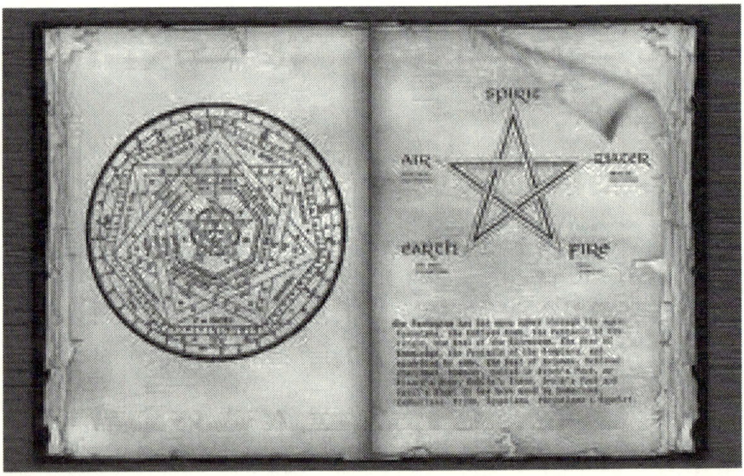
SPIRIT
AIR
WATER
EARTH
FIRE

Initiation Ritual

A Solitary Ritual

Initiation is a rite of passage ceremony marking entrance or acceptance into a group or society. Initiation denotes acceptance and implies that the student or disciple agrees to the requirements (such as living an ethical lifestyle, meditating, etc.) otherwise, the individual may not be allowed to participate in ceremonies or even in social ritual.

Mircea Eliade depicts initiation as a principle religious act. He defines initiation as *"a basic change in existential condition,"* which liberates us from profane time and history. He describes it as a body of rites and teachings whose purpose is to produce a decisive alteration in both the religious and the social status of the initiate. *"Initiation recapitulates the sacred history of the world. And through this recapitulation, the whole world is sanctified anew... [the initiate] can perceive the world as a sacred work, a creation of the Gods."*

The challenge or ordeal of initiation, and there must be such a beginning, measures the initiate's worthiness to enter the new status. Your ordeal will include a test of your courage in following this new path, and your fidelity to the principles involved. There must also be an oath, sometimes a vow of secrecy. Seclusion, a symbolic representation of death and rebirth, special instruction, and restrictions on the initiate are frequent additions to such ceremonies.

We will celebrate your spirit journey on various levels of purification at all levels of the experience (body, mind, emotions, and soul) in magical and mystical ways.

You will be tempered by what you must release in order to take this important step. Your willingness to surrender these things or habits requires a maturity of mind. This can only be developed by the practice of doing without, not by words alone. You must be willing to step into the unknown, away from the comfort zone you've built around you.

You will come closer to your spiritual deities than you ever imagined. Up till now, you have called upon deity, which is simply, prayer. To call upon deity within a sacred ceremony is ritual. Now, you will become one with deity, in a way that changes your concept of divinity, and that is initiation.

It is not necessary that you be disrobed at any point in this ritual, as the divine energies will enter you easily due to your preparation and intention, clothed or not. The choice is yours.

Your innermost thoughts

During the week previous to the initiation, you will keep a daily journal, in which you will record your meditations on the step you are about to take. Pay close attention to your dreams during this week, as many clues to your magical path will enter your mind in that state, and record any significant dreams in your journal.

You will also consider the many things, habits and thought processes you will release from yourself at the moment of initiation. Be certain that you are ready to relinquish these things without grief.

A magical name

You might also determine a magical name. Your new name, by which you will be known in your spiritual life from now on, should be fully recorded in the diary. Make note of the reasons for your choice, how you arrived at it, and any other bits of information pertinent to the name as you write. This name can one that has come to you in a dream, or one you've studied that resonates with you in a special way, or from any of several sources. It would be presumptuous to take on a title as well as a name, like "Lord" or "Lady". Those kinds of designations are usually reserved for elders, teachers, or priests and priestesses, and until you possess the proper credentials, you shouldn't presume to give yourself the title. If you decide to use a magical name in ritual, use it every time you work. Use it when you pray. You may even wish to perform a name ritual as part of your initiation, or just before it. A name ritual would consist of invoking the deity to recognize you by your new name. Using a magical name may not give you any additional power, but it's a traditional practice, and many enjoy it. Some seekers choose to be known by a magical name for the purposes of anonymity, perhaps using the name only in the public sector and not in magical work at all. If that is your choice, be sure to record that information as well. One last thing about names: if you are dedicated to a particular deity, do not presume to call yourself by that deity's name. Instead, find a developed formation of the divine name and use that. For instance, a follower of Apollo might be Apollonius or even Apollonia; or a follower of Diana (who was born on the island of Delos) might be Delia.

Final preparation

You will have prepared for your initiation by fasting for three days, in which you consume only water. This is the first stage of your ordeal. It will be difficult, but if it were easy, it wouldn't be an ordeal.

Having bathed yourself, both physically and magically, in preparation for this sacred journey, you will sit in vigil for three full hours, just before the ritual is to begin, pondering the importance of the step you are taking, while cleansing your mind and spirit of all fear or concern, encouraging yourself. This is the second stage of your ordeal. One more stage awaits you, within the ritual circle.

The ritual begins

After you have placed the boundaries of your worship circle, by whatever means you are most comfortable with, you will need to raise power. It is hoped that by the time you are ready to be initiated, you will have learned to raise power in a solitary aspect. You might learn to do this by concentrating or willing your power to be released. You might use physical motion to stir up energy, like walking swiftly around the circle, dancing or even just running. Some witches are able to raise power with intensive chanting. The raising of power is the third and final stage of your ordeal. Should you attempt to raise power by concentrating your will, it will be important that you do not doze.

When you feel that you have the energy built up inside you, and you are ready to release it, bring your projective hand (the one you write with) and visualizing the energy pouring out of you, place your hand over your head, your third eye, your heart or your stomach. The placement is wherever you feel is appropriate for you. At the top of your head, you are pouring power into your spirituality, and your aspirations. At the third eye, between your eyebrows, the power will benefit your intuition, insight and psychic abilities. Pouring the power into your heart benefits your ability to love, to feel compassion, self-control and self-acceptance. Power in your stomach area influences thought, intellect and your sense of self-confidence.

Wherever you've chosen to use the power, feel the energy coming out of your hand and becoming a part of your firm intention.

Empowered, you will speak to the deity, recounting the matters you are willing to release from your being. These can be offenses you feel you have committed, habits you've formed, or even just a longing to return to the deity.

You will then partake of the sacred meal, the cakes or bread, and the wine or water, having requested the Gods' blessings upon them before you consume them.

You will take an oath

Finally you will intone your intention to serve the deity, being specific as to how you will serve, how deeply you are willing to follow your commitment, etc. This is a strictly personal oath, but your oath should include...

- A solemn recitation of the reason for this ritual;
- the fact that your will in this matter is firm;
- a declaration of your intention to be one with the deity;
- a vow to keep the matters that have been revealed to you away from those who would seek to ridicule or berate you;
- your further study plans;
- a reflection of your attitude toward others you meet along your path;
- and a vow to maintain the secrecy of the true identity of your fellow travelers, if they require it, that they may not suffer due to your lapses.

You will write your own oath, in your own words and record it in your journal. You are permitted to read it from that source, if you wish.

Welcoming

A Child Blessing Ritual

Welcoming is a pagan ceremony or ritual similar to a christening or baptism for an infant in which the infant is presented to the God and Goddess. It is a first rite of passage for a new life. In the Wiccan traditions, this is called Wiccaning, but similar ceremonies are celebrated in other Neopagan religions as well. In those cases, while the format may resemble Wiccaning, it might be referred to as a Saining, a Blessing, or even a Witchering. (The word 'sain' is from Middle English, around the 12th century, derived from the Old English word *segnian*, which in turn derives from the Latin *signare*, meaning 'to mark It is used to mean 'bless' or even 'sign', as in the Middle Ages it was used to denote the making of the sign of the cross.)

A Welcoming is an opportunity for parents to present their Child to the five elements, requesting a blessing. Sometimes both the Child's legal name and the Child's ceremonial name are used, until such time as the Child chooses another name for themselves, usually at a coming of age. However, the parents may choose to use only the Child's legal name or only the ceremonial name they have chosen for the infant.

In accordance with the importance of free will in pagan traditions, the infant is not *expected* to choose a Pagan path for themselves when they grow older. In fact, the ceremony is focused on the parents' beliefs and the family's commitment to look after the Child. The ceremony is a remembrance that the Child has *chosen* to be born to the parents; it is a naming ceremony, and a time for the parents to express their feelings. Welcoming is also a ritual which allows everyone present a chance to speak their feelings and wishes, too. Should the baby cry during the ritual, don't worry, s/he is just participating!

The night before the ritual, sprinkle a circle of flax seed around the baby's sleeping area to protect and begin the blessing (not in the bed itself, but around it).

On the day of the ritual, bathe the baby in a warm bath that has a piece of elder wood in it. (Alternatively, you could place a handful of elder flower blossoms in a muslin bag to float in the baby's bath water).

Those who will participate in the ritual are asked to write a short blessing for the Child, which they will read aloud in the circle, and commit the paper to the flame. They are also to bring any symbolic gifts they wish to present to the Child. This is not required and need not be something costly or traditional like toys or clothing. The gift could be a poem, a gemstone, a collection of photographs or something the person made for the child. These things will be saved so that the child can have them again at a later age, to see all the wishes people had for them. Some examples might be: "*I bring this book and candle to you, in the hope your intellect will burn brightly;*" "*I bring this teddy bear to you, hopes that you will feel safe and comfortable throughout your childhood;*" "*I bring this song to you, to bless you with an appreciation of music,*" etc.

The Child will have Goddess parents for this ritual, carefully chosen by the parents. The Goddess Parents' job is not only to help in the naming and blessing of the child, but to provide it with the magic tools it can use once it reaches adulthood. These can be the symbolic gifts they bring to the Child.

Setting up the ritual area

The Goddess-parents assist the Priest and Priestess in drawing the circle upon the ground. Using five (5) different media, they outline a five-pointed star, six (6) feet wide, on the ground. (Suggested media include: salt, flour, beans, seeds, fairy dust, coffee, dried herbs, etc.; any product that can be sprinkled loosely and will be readily visible to the participants.) Using salt that has been blessed, they next trace a circle around the star and another, three (3) feet outside it. The guests will be instructed to stand within the two circles. A chair has been placed at each point of the star, within the two circles, to accommodate the grandparents and other family members, if attending. The main altar is placed in the center. There, candles await, along with a special white candle representing the Child, into which the Child's name has been carved. Also on the altar are whatever representations the parents wish to symbolize for this occasion. Symbols of the moon and sun are also there (a simple moon mask and sun mask would work well, since the parents will become these celestial bodies at a point of the ritual). Room should be left for other articles that will accumulate during the ritual. There, also, is the bread/cake product that will be consumed and the wine/ale/water product as well. An athame should be there, even if it is not needed to cut the bread, as a symbol of the division (and sharing) of food. A medium-sized, handled basket lies at the foot of the altar.

Chairs are placed in the center of the circle to accommodate both parents. They have done much work, bringing this Child into the world, and they are to rest during the first part of the ceremony, holding the Child.

At each point of the star, a small altar is set, to hold the workings of each of the elements, within the inner circle. At the first, Air, a feather and incense are required. The second is Fire, and requires a sacrificial bowl in which paper may be burned and the tools required to complete the sacrifice, along with a candle. Next is Water, and there should be warmed water in a blue bowl and a seashell to sprinkle it. Then, Earth, where a very small drum should be. Last is Spirit, and a bell and a length of silver thread, are placed there. Colors and additional artifacts are left to the parents' own preferences.

Within the Pentagram will stand the Mother (seated), Father (seated), Child (held by the parents), God-father, Goddess-mother and the Priest and Priestess. The grandparents and any aunts, uncles, cousins, etc., if attending, are to be seated - with honor - at the intervals of the star's points. All motion within the circle is deosil.

Have baby oil on hand to moisten the child's third eye before applying any milkweed juice as an anointing medium. Alternatively, you could simply use almond oil or olive oil for the anointing.

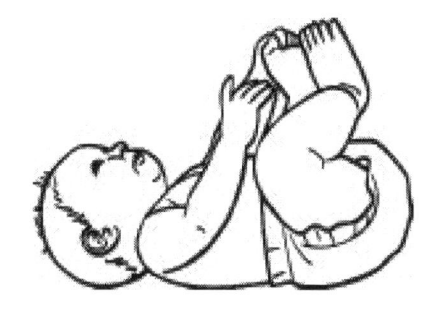

The ritual begins

Suggested music: The Witch Song, by Anne Hill, (Circle Round and Sing! - Serpentine Music Productions)

The Priest and Priestess are the first to enter the circle and to dedicate it. They anoint and welcome the Goddess parents, who now welcome the guests into the outer circle, anointing them with baby oil, saying, *"Welcome to this sacred space. Enter in and feel the grace."* The parents and the Child should be the last to enter the circle, proceeding into the inner circle. A brief, general greeting is offered to the guests by the parents, in their own words.

The Priestess lights the Child's candle and speaks the Child's name aloud to the gods for the first time.

The Gatherer (a child of 9 years, but not more than 13) holds the sacrificial bowl, which has been taken from the fire altar temporarily, while the Goddess-parents each state aloud a wish/blessing for the Child, crumpling the paper on which it is written and placing it in the bowl. The bowl is then held for the first guest, who will read the wish s/he has written, crumple the paper and add it to the sacrifice bowl. Someone in the circle has been asked to record the wishes as they are read aloud, which are saved for the Child's Witching Book. The Gatherer continues around the outer circle until all the guests who wish to have contributed a sacrifice to the bowl. When the wishes have all been read, the bowl is returned to the Fire altar.

The Priest and Priestess visit the Child in the parent's arms, for the initial blessing.

Priestess: *May your life be divine; and may all the blessings of the Universe bestow upon you."*

The Priest, using the juice of the milkweed herb, anoints the Child on the third eye, saying: *I awaken your imagination and your creative powers.*

Presenting to Air

The Priest, Priestess, God-father, Goddess-mother and Gatherer, who now carries the empty basket that was at the foot of the altar, take the Child (carried by the Goddess-parents) and proceed to the first point of the Pentagram, the Air altar, where the God-father lights the incense.

Priest: "*In the element of air, we discover you, (name) who has returned to us in a new body, initiated into this lifetime on (date of the Child's birth), by your chosen Mother. Your chosen Father awaited your arrival, enchanted. Your gift to us is our joy, and we radiate it back to you with our love and our words.*"

Suggested Music: Wherever You Go by Lady Bridget and the Belladonnas (Voices of the Goddess)

Placing a feather in the smoke of the incense and brushing the tip of it across the Child's head and face, the Priestess continues, "*In the breath of scent, I capture wings of thought intelligent; These gifts declare the element of air.*" The feather is then placed in the basket held by the Gatherer.

Goddess-mother: "*Forces of air, I present (name) to you for your inspection and your protection.*"

Presenting to Fire

The entire group proceeds to the Fire altar, where a candle is lit by the Goddess-mother and the wishes in the bowl are set aflame.

Priestess: "*Through the element of fire we guide you, (name), who reminds us of the fervor of youth. As you begin to explore this world and your place in it, may all these wishes enrich your journey. The courage and creativity* you will manifest will help you expand your capabilities, transpose your frailties and celebrate your humanity."

Suggested Music: Little One by Lady Bridget (In Her Sacred Space)

Anointing the Child with the ashes of the blessings, the Priest continues, "*In the passion of flame I proclaim the spark of life in you is rife. These gifts inspire the element of fire.*" The ashes are collected into a small container and placed in the basket.

God-father: "*Forces of fire, I present (name) to you for your inspection and your protection.*"

Presenting to Water

The group proceeds to the Water altar. The Priest says, "*With the element of water, we accept you, (name), who has entered our hearts and will lead us in the perfection of our love. Your depth of knowing is boundless and you find power in peace. These will guide your search for a path of living.*"

Suggested Music: Rain Song by Anne Hill (Circle Round and Sing! Serpentine Music Productions)

Dipping a seashell into the water, the Priestess 'washes' the Child's feet, saying, "*I wash your feet, to make them sweet; May this element bless you with tolerance.*" The seashell is added to the basket.

Goddess-mother: "*Forces of water, I present (name) to you for your inspection and your protection.*"

Presenting to Earth

At the Earth altar, the Priestess says, "*On the element of earth, we stand at a crossroad with you, (name), who brings transition into many lives with your coming. The strength of your body connects you to the planet on which we stand. You were born with a purpose and we are honored to serve your birth-vision.*"

Suggested Music: Teach Me by Lady Bridget (In Her Sacred Space)

Taking the Child's hand, the Priest aids him/her to beat the small drum, at least once, saying, "*As you sound the drum of endless being, you are a part of everything; I bless your birth with the element of earth.*" The drum is added to the basket.

God-father: "*Forces of earth, I present (name) to you for your inspection and your protection.*"

Presenting to Spirit

Finally, at the Spirit altar, the Priest says, "*In the spirit of element, we welcome you, (name), whose quest blesses our own journey; whose promise will change the world in which we live. The path you will one day choose will enable you to answer the questions that arise from your soul.*"

Suggested Music: Heat of Our Heart's Desire by Anne Hill (Circle Round and Sing! Serpentine Music Productions)

The Priestess rings a bell, and it, too, is added to the basket.

Goddess-mother: "*Spirit of eternity, I present (name) to you for your inspection and your protection.*"

Goddess parents devotion

As the god/goddess-parents hold the Child, the Priestess takes a length of silver thread and circles round them three times, saying, *"(Name), your spiritual wonder is placed in the safekeeping of your Goddess-mother, (name) and your God-father, (name). I bind that part of you to their care."*

While still bound, the god/goddess-parents devote themselves to the Child with these words:

Speaking together: *"As above, so below; As the universe, so the soul; As without, so within;*
Blessed (name), on this day, at this moment, I dedicate myself to your spirit
God-father only: *with my body will I protect you,*
Goddess-mother only: *with my mind will I enlighten you,*
God-father only: *with my spirit will I guide you,*
Goddess-mother only: *until you shall choose your own path.*
Speaking together: *So mote it be."*

Suggested Music: Our Ways by Lady Bridget (In Her Sacred Space)

The binding is removed and saved in the basket, which is again placed at the foot of the altar. The Gatherer is released from the inner circle and takes a place in the outer circle.

The parents begin to participate

The group returns to the center altar where the mother and father await. Mother holds the Child while father stands, portraying himself as the Sun, and gives the Sun's blessing:

*"May the golden light from beyond this earth
Fill you, surround you and enlighten your waking moments
all the days of your life."*

Father now holds the Child while mother stands, portraying herself as the Moon, and gives the Moon's blessing:

*"May the silver light reflected upon this earth
Soothe you, embrace you and enlighten your inner self all
the days of your life."*

The Priestess now offers her blessing/wish for the Child, as the parents hold him/her. *"(Name), your ordeal is nearly ended. Lay now in the arms of love, for your journey, once begun, will take you far. Remember to begin within, for if that which you seek you cannot find within, you will never find it without."*

Naming the child

The parents sit or stand in the center of the circle with the baby, for the empowerment. The Priestess begins, simply chanting the Child's name, and the others will start to say it in different ways, some whispering, some singing, or just saying it in different tones, so that it makes a musical sound that raises protective energy. When the power is at its peak, the Mother and Father should call it by holding the Child aloft as the energy goes forth to the universe, identifying the presence of the Child.

The energy is part of a protective shield for the Child. As part of that, the Priest would step forward, touch the Child, and say: *"Your very name protects you from all harm. The sound of it forbids physical or psychic hurt. This is the Charm."*

The Priestess touches the Child and says: *"Your true name is the shield you wear against evil. Its music grants you peace and serenity against upheaval."*

Suggested Music: Door to Fairie by Lady Bridget (In Her Sacred Space)

The Sacred Meal

The Priestess consecrates the bread/cake/wafers, held by the Goddess-parents, saying, *"This bread of life feeds our bodies and our minds, sustains us through our time on this earth. Flesh of the earth, I consecrate you for the nourishment of this gathering!"*

A crumb of the bread is brushed against the Child's mouth*, as the Priestess says: *May you never hunger, lest it be for freedom, and then, may you never have enough...*

She partakes of the wafer, offers it to the Priest, the Goddess-parents and the parents, then the god/goddess-parents pass the plate to feed all within the outer circle.

The Priest next consecrates fresh water, held by the Goddess-parents, saying, *"This wine of creation satisfies, showers our bodies and our spirits, floods us with the melody of eternity. Blood of the earth, I charge you, make this a potion of purest magic!"*

A drop of the water is brushed against the Child's mouth, as the Priest says: *May you never thirst, lest it be for knowledge, and then, may you never be filled...*

He partakes of the water, passing it to the Priestess, then the Goddess-parents, who also partake, then pass it to the parents and all within the outer circle.

*If the child is old enough, the food and drink may be offered for consumption by the child, but if it is an infant, the touch of the food and drink on the baby's lips is sufficient.

The Community

When the guests have been served and all have consumed the food and drink, Mother and Father introduce, by name and relationship to the Child, each of the special guests in the outer circle. The parents travel deosil around the edge of the inner circle, allowing each of the guests to see the Child and present any small gifts they may have brought for the occasion. These gifts are collected by the parents and added to the Child's memory basket.

Suggested Music: Magickal Child by Lady Bridget and the Belladonnas (Voices of the Goddess)

The Closing

The Priest begins to close the ceremony: *"We are grateful for the presence of the forces of air, water, fire, earth and spirit, who have attended us here to welcome this blessed Child. Return now to your sacred places with our appreciation."*

The Priestess offers her closing: *"What is, was, and what was, is. The circle is open, yet it is unbroken.
Merry meet, merry part and merry meet again."*

The items in the basket that were collected during the ritual are the Child's mementos of the occasion.

Suggested Music: When You're Magic by Anne Hill (Circle Round and Sing! Serpentine Music Productions)

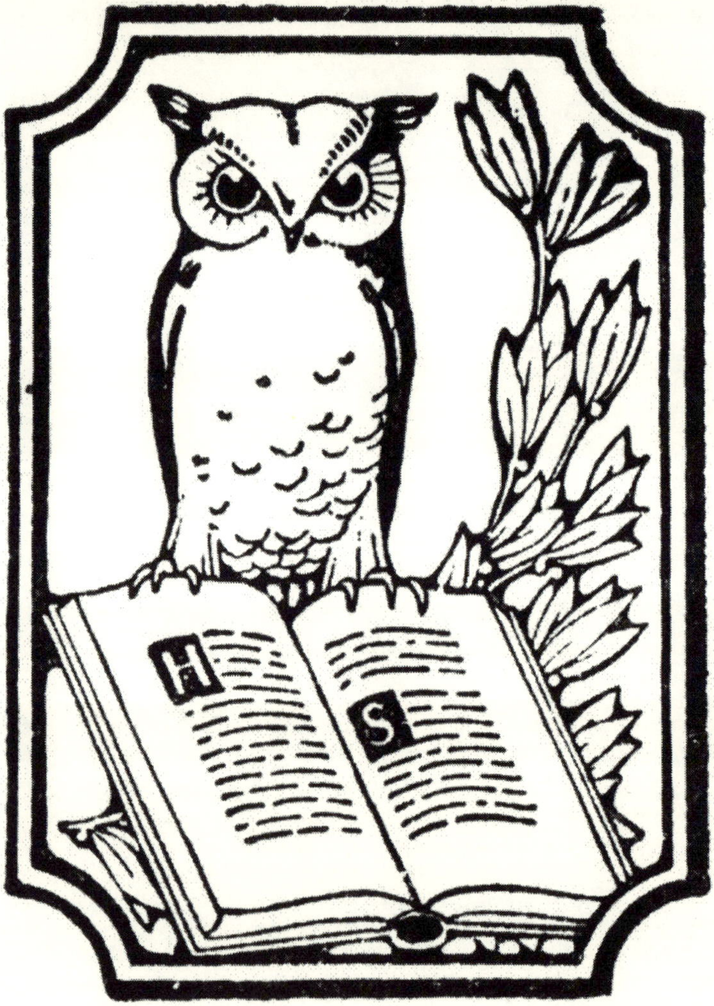

House Blessing Ritual

Set up an altar in the entry area of the house. If there is no specific entry area, set the altar as close to the front door as possible, without blocking traffic. On this altar, you will have a candle, a mechanism to light the candle at the proper time, a container of blessed salt, another container of blessed water and a small bowl of pure oil (I use extra-virgin olive oil) and a sprig of fresh basil. You will also have bread, wine, and a chalice to drink from, and a small mirror.

During this ritual you will navigate the entire house three times, traveling in a clockwise direction at all times. Each journey will begin and end at the altar. It is suggested that all the members of the household be present at this ritual, and travel each leg of the journey with you, if possible.

To begin the ceremony, you will light the candle and invite the deity of your choice to attend the ritual, adding her or his energy to yours.

Take the container of blessed salt and begin to travel the various rooms. If the house is a two-story dwelling, begin at the top and work down. Otherwise, begin at the room to the right of the altar and go on from there. At each inner doorway and each window, sprinkle some of the blessed salt, saying, *"I purify this portal. Let all negative energies depart this place and never return."*

When all the rooms have been purged with salt, you will find yourself back at the altar. Take, then, the container of blessed water, and begin the second leg of the journey. Again, at each inner doorway and every window, as well as in every corner of every room (including closets), sprinkle a few drops of the water, saying, *"May no harmful energies cross this portal, nor dwell in these corners."*

Once more, you find yourself back at the altar. This time, take up the bowl of oil and the sprig of basil. Travel the rooms in the same order once more, and, using the basil as an asperger (sprinkler), barely dip it into the oil, and sprinkle the center of each room and closet and hallway, saying, *"May love, happiness, friendship, prosperity and peace abound in this place."* Be stingy with the oil, or there will have to be a large clean-up afterward.

Back at the altar, take the wine, and anoint all the external thresholds, front, rear, and any other entrances or exits of the house, with a few drops of wine, saying, *"Grant entry to all friends and loved ones, but turn aside all who would do harm within."*

At the altar, the small mirror should be hung in such a way as to reflect anyone passing through the front door. This doesn't need to be obvious, but it must catch the reflection of all visitors.

Now you will begin the general prayer of protection for the house and household:

Every window, every door

*from the ceiling to the floor;
every paint and papered wall,
every corner, large or small,
cleansèd now of all that harm,
hearken to my sacred charm.
Bless the beds to give them rest,
family, friend and even guest;
Bless the table filled with food,
never hunger is the rood;
Bless the chair that comfort brings
to peasants and as well to kings
Bless the hearth to warm them too,
may their dreaming all come true.
Those who choose to stay within,
may you be a paladin:
guard the folk who here reside,
let their joy and love abide.*

Now you may bless and share the bread and wine with all the members of the household, to ground the work that has been completed.

Thank the deity and blow out the candle. The ritual is ended.

Croning Ritual

This ritual is to be performed at or just before the new moon

It was written especially for my eldest daughter, when she felt the time was right.

Each woman to be croned will have determined what are her symbols of maidenhood, motherhood and cronehood. The cronehood symbol is to be worn on her head, but not until the proper time in the ceremony. We have presumed the symbol of maidenhood to be a red scarf, worn loosely at her neck at the beginning of the ceremony, and will be tied at her waist later. The motherhood symbol must also be something she can wear. Each of these symbols will be for her to wear ever after, especially during rituals, as evidence of her progression through the triplicity of life. The symbols are on the altar, waiting for the correct time to be placed on the celebrant. Cakes and beverage are waiting on the altar for the sacred meal.

Also on the altar is a grouping of three stones, blessed salt, a new journal and pen, and a staff (decorated by the celebrant) which will be presented to her later in the ritual.

On a table near the celebrant, she will have brought small symbolic gifts that she will present to her guests later in the ritual; these items can be as simple as a card that recognizes their attendance at the croning. There also is water (or fairy dust) which she will sprinkle on the dancers. This table will receive any material gifts and symbolic memories brought by the guests.

The circle is set with a large container in the center, which holds water. This could be simply a cauldron, or even a small 'wishing' well, which contains water. The outer edge of the 9-foot circle is planted with chairs and/or floor cushions for the guests to sit upon. Noise makers are left near each sitting area, and can include rattles, bells, and drums. A 'throne" is set up in front of the altar for the celebrant. This is to be a Comfortable Circle.

The scribing and blessing of the circle is to be done according to the tradition chosen by the celebrant, with only the Priestess and the celebrant within it. The visitors remain outside the circle until they are invited in by the celebrant.

Priestess: *Have you laid aside the erupting passions of your past, to replace them with the robust passions of your future?*

The Celebrant answers.

Priestess: *Are you prepared to receive the wisdom of the crones of ancient days?*

The Celebrant answers.

Priestess: *Who supports you here?*

Those the celebrant has invited specially to witness her croning, ages 10 and up, pagan or not are formally invited by her to enter the circle, by name. Each guest is anointed as they enter. When they have all entered and are seated around the circle, they are invited to speak for the first time.

Priestess: *Each of these present will please speak a word sharing her memories of this woman...*

(A short story-telling ensues, in which each guest is invited to tell a memory or why this woman is special.)

Priestess presents the three stones to the celebrant, saying:

These stones represent your life - past, present and future. It matters not which is which, for all is interconnected. Love, friendship and respect are represented here, and maiden, mother and crone as well. The following recitation can be spoken by chosen guests.

In your lifetime,

You asked for Strength...
And Goddess gave you difficulties to make you strong.

You asked for Wisdom...
And Goddess gave you problems to solve.

You asked for Prosperity...
And Goddess gave you a brain and brawn to work.

You asked for Courage...
And Goddess gave you obstacles to overcome.

You asked for Love...
And Goddess gave you troubled people to help.

You asked for Favors...
And Goddess gave you opportunities.

You received nothing you wanted...
But You received everything you needed.

The Priestess lights the first wick of a triple-wick candle...
Priestess: *You began as a maiden*
When the living river of blood became a part of you
And opened your creative powers.
(The red scarf is removed from her neck and is tied at her waist)

The Priestess lights the second wick of the candle...
Priestess: *You became a mother*
Birthing life in many forms: a child, ideas, art, passion, and more than these,
As the flowing river wound its way through you.
(The motherhood symbol is placed on her)

The Priestess lights the third wick of the candle...

Priestess: *Now you have come full circle*
And you are the living goddess, incarnate.
The river of blood has followed you and moved on.
(The crone symbol is placed on her)

The celebrant is asked to stand, and blessed salt is sprinkled upon and around her feet

Priestess: *You are the salt of the earth. You enrich and preserve all the flavors of life.*

Priestess: *Will you accept the crown of ages upon your warrior brow?*

The celebrant answers
(The crown is placed on her head)

Priestess: *Maiden, Mother, Crone, all exist in you. You are one with the universe, from now until forever.*

The staff of cronehood is presented to the crone.

The crone leads a Walk with the Wise, all around the circle, slowly, three times. A suggested chant is from Kellianna, "I Walk With the Goddess", uplifting and simple, the words are true to this celebration.

The crone then retires to her throne to watch as the others perform for her benefit, with music, dancing, singing, etc., as they have planned for this occasion, raising power which they will direct to the new crone. Those who do not care to join the dancing may take their seats at the outer edge of the circle, and are asked to clap, chant, sing, or make joyful noise for the benefit of the dancers. The music for the dancing will have been chosen beforehand for its energy.

The crone may randomly sprinkle the dancers with water (in a mist form) from the center well, or with fairy dust, as she prefers, while they dance.

The cakes and ale are blessed, and given first to the crone, then the priestess, then shared with the guests, served by the youngest visitants. The crone has determined ahead of time whom she wishes to lead this part of the ritual.

Eat now with the Goddess, as She becomes your present.
May you never hunger, lest it be for freedom,
May you never have enough.

Drink now with the Goddess, as She enters your consciousness.
May you never thirst, lest it be for knowledge,
May you never slake that thirst.

The new crone stands and the red scarf is used (by the eldest member of the group) to embrace the crone lightly, breezily, as it is drawn across her shoulders and dropped onto the earth.

Elder: *The goddess has released you from the flowing river of blood,*
That living sacrifice which can only be offered by a woman,
And yet your power remains – female and strong.
No more will your body prepare to receive life,
And yet you are a temple of life,
No more will you bring life from your body,
Now life springs only from your heart and mind.

The youngest member of the group presents a new journal and pen to the crone...

Maiden: *For the next year and a day, you will receive goddess wisdom from the crones,*
The great ones and the common ones.
Be open to their teachings.
Pay attention, for they will approach you in many guises.
They will find you in your dreams, in your memories, and in your reveries.
Let them write your history in their hearts,
Let them write your future in yours.

Priestess: *Are you willing to share the wisdom you have amassed through this lifetime?*

The crone answers and the gifts from the crone to her guests are distributed

Priestess: *Now the wisdom of the ages will enter you*
Through Minerva, Athena,
Through the crones who have come before you
And those who stand with you now,
For the goddess has accepted your years of sacrifice
And she rejoices in you.

Priestess: *Come, friends and well-wishers, come forward and present your wishes, your memories and your salutations to the crone.*

The crone, enthroned, receives each guest once more, as they offer her their wishes for her future. If the guests have brought symbolic gifts or memorabilia, they may bring them forward at this time, or each guest can give of themselves, presenting a song, a dance, a poem. This should be a joyful, whimsical event, with wishes that bring laughter and entertainment for everyone.

Priestess: *Above you, the stars…*
Below you, the stones…
Behind you, the tears…
Before you, the laughter.
As time passes, remember,
Like a star, your wisdom should be enlightening.
Like a stone, your wisdom should be patient.
Like a tear, your wisdom can be salty.
Like a laugh, your wisdom must be heartfelt.

The new crone carries a container of water, taken from the well, around the circle's edge, sprinkling it, and blessing it while releasing the boundaries of the circle to the elements.

Priestess: *You are now the ruler of your own inner realms. You are forever invited to make known your understanding of life and to lend your wisdom to enlighten others to life's beauty and its ugliness, its light and shadow; for the awakened woman is ruler of her own life. So mote it be.*

The ritual is ended and the circle is opened, according to the tradition chosen by the crone.

Witch's Tea

This ritual is best held on a Saturday evening at a Dark moon, the Crone's Moon.

Groundwork, at least a week in advance

Have anointing oil made up and placed at all entrances. A recipe is included at the end of this ritual.

Prepare the entire house magically, by cleansing every corner of every room; Set up all protections against evil and negative influences; Set up small altars, one in each room.

Evoke the Goddess to take residence within the walls of the house, for a sacred ritual is to take place there, honoring Her.

Have two sets of cards printed and handy to give guests at the proper time.
The first card says: *"Look at the stars above you. Each star represents a positive attribute that exists in you. Name each of those attributes and claim them as your own, in perfect silence."*
The second card says: *"Light the tea-light you were given and silently name the things that interfere with your spiritual growth in the flame; example: my fear. Meditate upon the following in perfect silence. As the candle burns so does (my fear); When it dies, (my fear) ceases to be.*

You will have placed glow-in-the-dark stars on the ceiling of the room where the ritual is to take place.
You will have tea lights, one for each guest, ready to distribute at the beginning of the ritual.
You will also have small bottles of bubbles ready to distribute for the last part of the ritual.
Set the area with the teapot and tea caddy, tea ball, cups and saucers with spoons. Have milk, lemon and sweeteners handy for tea. The tea you use can be ordinary tea, or an herbal tea of your own making, or even a blend of both. If you have no tea ball, be sure to have a tea strainer handy when pouring or some cups will be filled with leaves and very little tea.
Have an offering bowl and a waste bowl with a cover. You will also need boiling water, and a container to hold a pot-full of hot water, after

the pot has been heated.

On the Day of the Ritual

Appoint a Guardian to be placed at the door against late entries. They are to be admitted, silently, if they arrive before the tea is set to steep. After that, they must watch silently from afar, until the music begins once again.

Each guest will be anointed with the oil on her third eye, as she enters the house, saying: *Welcome goddess, be at peace*

Have guests put all cell phones on vibrate or turn them off during ritual. Phones are NOT to be answered during the ritual.

The ritual begins

Turn off all the electric lights.
Light all the working candles, but not the large triple-wick candle.
Give each guest a tea-light, and place matches nearby.

"Do not light these little lights just yet, wait until you are instructed to do so."

Be certain the guests have calmed, and are paying attention to you and not the ceiling.

"No circle will be drawn for this ritual, because the entire space has been prepared for it and is sacred. Some of this ritual is done is absolute silence, because the dark moon is a time of meditation, reflection and silence; a time of new beginnings, new commitments and new projects. Therefore, when the music stops, all speaking must cease, and no whispering is to be heard."

The Goddess is invited

"Beloved Goddess, we invite You to accompany us this evening as we attend to our own inner Goddess, partaking of a blessed tea with You. We release ourselves into Your care for the time we are silent. Guard and guide us through the darkness of that silence, that we may emerge from it whole and healed of all earthly discord. Welcome to Your place in our lives."

"The Goddess is around us and within us. She is immanent and transcendent. She represents the divine embodied in nature, in human beings, in the flesh."

Light a triple-wick candle.

"The triple-wick candle represents the triple goddess, whom we honor here tonight."
"When the music begins to play again, you may speak, but not a word must be heard until then."

Turn the music off.

Make the Tea

Fill the pot with boiling water, and empty it out, to warm the pot.
Fill the tea ball with tea and place it into the pot.
Fill the pot with boiling water.
Place a cozy over the pot to keep it warm while it steeps. If you have no tea cozy, you may place a folded towel over the pot, loosely, just to maintain its heat.

First pursuit

Distribute the first cards telling the guests what to do next:
Allow at least 10 minutes for the tea to steep and the activity to conclude.
First, pour a drop of tea into the offering bowl. Pour and distribute the tea to the guests.

Second endeavor

Distribute the second card telling the guests what to do next:
Allow at least 10 to 15 minutes for the activity to conclude.

Silence ends, and the third encounter begins.
Turn the music on.

"Thank you for your silence; now we are able to speak freely."

Distribute small bottles of bubbles.
"These bubbles are for the third activity of this ritual. As you blow a bubble, you are to name it for a problem or stumbling block in your life. You may do this silently or aloud, if you like. Watch that named bubble waft away from you, then burst and disappear."

Allow enough time for everyone to be fully involved and enjoy this part of the ritual. This is a fun time, so you might want to allow at least 20 minutes or more. Be sure the music is lively and positive.

Thank the Goddess:
"Beloved Goddess, we release You from this ritual, and we thank you for attending our ritual this evening as we healed our own inner Goddess. Our wholeness is one with Yours. We have grown with You in our silent time, while You have protected us through the darkness of that silence. Stay with us in celebration if You wish, or go if You must. This space is always Yours."

Now is the time to eat and drink and Share recipes/spells/rituals.

Wise Resolutions

A New Year's Ritual

Making New Year's resolutions has become a rather tired and useless diversion. The idea is still sound, but we seem to lose our focus after a very short time. Perhaps we need to update the manner in which we set these resolutions. Maybe making a true ritual of the process will allow us to retain our motivation a bit longer....

Cast a circle around a writing table, set with paper and writing implements, and enough room for all invited guests to participate at the same time.

At the writing table, allow time for each person to consider the following matters:

What worked really well during the previous year?

What didn't work as well as we would have liked? Or was a disappointment?

What did you accomplish that you are really proud of?

What choices did you make that you now know were wrong for you?

What changes do you still feel you need in your life?

After considering the answers to the preceding questions, they are instructed to begin to write their resolutions.

Remind your guests to be realistic about their chances of succeeding with these resolutions. People often do themselves a bad turn by hatching plans for self-change that are unreasonable - their expectations are far too high and they're making it hard on themselves. They're underestimating the power of their habits. When they realize they're not meeting their goals they become frustrated and despondent. Make sure the goals are realistic.

The most common resolutions people make include: to lose weight, to stop smoking, to save money, to exercise. Unfortunately each of these, although admirable aspirations, are quite vague. In order for a resolution to have a chance at success, it must be specific. For instance, resolve to become a non-smoker by the end of the new year. This gives you 12 months to get to that fabulous goal, removing the pressure of getting it done immediately. If you want to resolve to exercise, and you don't indulge in any exercise at all as the year begins, you could try exercising once a week, for only 30 minutes each time, for the first month. As the second month comes along, you might add another 30 minutes each week, on a different day. In the third month, you might want to add a different type of exercise to the program you are already following - perhaps a mile walk, in addition to the exercises you've been doing for the first two months. In this way, you will have developed a healthy exercise program by the end of the new year, that you didn't have to 'endure', and which will have become a consistent habit in the 12 months you've been practicing.

Therefore, you will break down your resolution(s) into a twelve-step program, with one step to be accomplished in each coming month. Again, be realistic. If any single step is too large or too difficult, you might feel disheartened when they can't accomplish it in the time allotted, and that is what makes you give up trying to keep your resolutions.

Every problem has small steps that can lead to big changes, and working them this way will allow the luxury of feeling successful at every step of the process. At the end of a year, you will have conquered your intention, and made a significant change in your life. A month may seem like a long time to focus on only one change, but I've found trying to change more than a few habits at a time to be reckless. With just one habit change, you can focus on making it really stick.

For instance, suppose your resolution is to try to be neater. You could start the first month by being sure to put things away while they are in your hand – like clothes, books, papers, food, etc. Putting it in the proper place right away avoids the difficulty of having to pick up *everything* at the same time, which can be exhausting, time-consuming, and cause you to feel like you've failed – again. The second step could be something as simple as providing a collection point in each room to hold things that don't belong in that room, so you can take everything out of the room at the same time, as you're leaving the room. Of course, you will continue the new habit you formed the first month, by putting things where they belong while they are in your hand, all through the second, third, and following months. You can see that each step, repeated over the whole month and the months afterward, will easily become a new habit, resulting in a neater you by the end of the year.

Tell the guests:
Begin to create the Resolution Plan by asking yourself why you want to

make this particular resolution.

Additional ideas for Resolution Rituals

The Talisman

A way to ensure that you don't forget your resolution is to create a talisman that will remind you of your good intentions every time you see it. A talisman draws good things to the wearer, and an amulet keeps other things away from the wearer. You will determine whether you require a talisman or an amulet for your resolution. It can be something really simple, as long as it continues to remind you of your plan. For instance, suppose your resolution is to work out more at the gym. Create a talisman that attaches to your gym clothes, or your gym bag.

Take your time making the talisman, and invoke your intentions into it as you work. It could be a pin with a particular design, a special button with words of encouragement on it, a pouch filled with herbs and stones, or any other item you feel is appropriate for you.

Preparing a talisman or an amulet with others helps to inform your memory that your friends and family are witness to your intentions, and will be supportive of your efforts. Once it is completed, you will take it to the altar where you and your magical sisters and brothers will come together to charge it, infuse it with the power you will need to follow your wishes. The combined power will help make it stronger than one you may have charged by yourself, and again, embraces the support of your friends and family.

Some habits are not bad habits, but are those you no longer need to retain in your life, as you are ready to move on without them. Some are simply habits that formed over time, while you were busily concentrating on other matters, and now must be addressed. Ideas abound for any kind of resolution you might choose. Ideas like...

An herb pillow for those who suffer insomnia and are determined to overcome it.
A pretty ring to grace a finger whose nail is never bitten again.
A necklace made of green beads and green ribbon, knotted nine times between the beads, to wear to encourage financial freedom.
A medal of 'courage' to wear as jewelry, against a fearful nature you wish to overcome.
A money jar to collect a small 'fine' when one uses a word or phrase they wish to banish from their language. This could also work for smokers trying to quit. The jar could be decorated with symbols of what you will spend all that money on when the year ends. You can fine yourself for continuing the habit, or commend yourself for not continuing.

Pros and Cons

Make a pro and con list for each habit you wish to convert. On the pro side, list the benefits of continuing to indulge in this habit, and on the con side, list what you are losing by continuing to indulge in it. Now you must determine whether the pros outweigh the cons. You will choose what you value more: the benefit or the loss. Each time you start to do whatever the bad habit is, now you have to actively choose. Which do you value more?

You will now make a choice to perform a better, alternative action in its place. What the new habit is that you substitute isn't so important as whether you feel good about the choices you have made.

Blended Waters

A fun game to play comes from Russia, by way of Judika Illes:

Each person must bring with them their own formula of magical water, or blessed water, or clear spring water. They can also bring a selection of small metal charms or rings, each symbolizing something. A cauldron will receive the ornaments. The host/ess can add a symbol appropriate to the group's pagan worship, perhaps a pentacle or a small goddess statuette. One by one, the guests approach the cauldron to empty their small container of water into it, while meditating on their wishes for the new year.

As all the waters have been emptied into the cauldron, the host/ess sprinkles it with mugwort and oats, or other herbs of choice. One lighted charcoal disc for each guest is now added to the cauldron. The host/ess stirs the cauldron with her or his non-power little finger, and the cauldron is covered.

Each guest comes forward, speaking a rhyme that relates to, but doesn't necessarily reveal their wish. When a verse is completed, the host/ess reaches into the cauldron and pulls out one charm to give the speaker, which will provide a clue to the success of that wish.

The blended waters should be immediately disposed of at an intersection when the ritual is ended, and should never be allowed to linger in the dwelling.

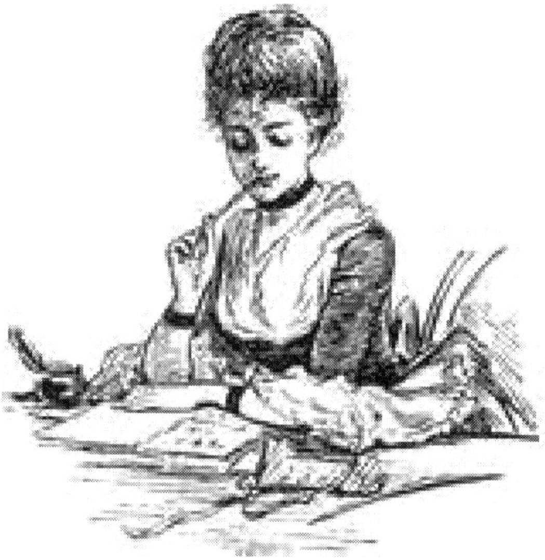

Womantide

A Menarche ritual in pastoral form

In the circle is a moon hut, an open frame 'house', with flowing white curtains instead of walls, very lightly attached, ready to be pulled down. Rolled up inside the top of the walls are sheer red curtains, waiting to be unfurled. A serpentine pathway of rose petals leads from the outer edge of the circle to the entrance of the moon hut.

The child to be honored is dressed in white. Her Sponsor (mother or guardian) is dressed in red. The Priestess is dressed in a fleshtone garment, which is decorated with leaves and flowers, and swirls of blue. She is representing the Earth. Her lipstick is bright red.

The Priest is dressed in white, with a leafy wreath on his head. A Male (the child's father or guardian) is present. Another Woman is also present, wearing something red. This can be a grandmother, an aunt, or any other elder female known to the child. Two Maidens are dressed in white garments with a red crescent moon on the front and the back; their shoes are red. The maidens should be known to the child, but older than she, and already menstruating.

You should have, at the ready, a tube of bright red lipstick, held by the Priestess; a red permanent marker, held by the Sponsor; a red feather, a lighted red candle, a seashell with a little water in it, a red clay bowl, honey and a dropper, salt, a dish of strawberries (or some other red fruit), a red drink in a chalice, and music for the dancing at the end.

The child is outside the moon hut/circle, as are the Priest and the male and the woman. The Priestess stands at one side of the circle. The Sponsor is on the other side, while the maidens are within the moon hut.

Priestess. *"Welcome to our celebration of naked bliss*
For this moment, a child receives her woman's kiss."

Sponsor, *"You are the beloved witness to our rite…*
Your faces will be our moonlight."

Priestess: *"You are the venerable community…*
Your presence gives us our reality."

Sponsor: *"You are the coven of universe…*

Our membership is truly diverse."

The Child begins to approach the moon hut, led by the Priest. The Male and the Woman come behind.

Priestess *"Comes the little girl, the child, the innocent,*
Comes she now to find her sacred element.
Childishness she leaves behind...
Today she welcomes womankind."

Child: *"Bring me all the wisdom of women's ages*
Let it attend me through these stages
May I drink deeply of Her lore
And be more wondrous than I was before."

Sponsor *"Let there be inspiration in this rite*
For the child becomes the maiden tonight."

Male *"Her very look a swarm of bees will kill,*
Blunt steel, make seeds go sterile.
In her presence wine will sour,
And withered is the bower.
She cannot put up vegetables or fruit,
For they will certainly pollute.
Butter will not come and bread will never rise,
Mirrors will go dim with a glance from her eyes."

Priest *"Nonsense, these are old wives' tales you say*
All are proven wrong in this our modern day.
Superstitions only are these things,
Let us not believe these blubberings."

Male *"They were facts in my time, I must tell you,*
And lasted centuries, so they must be true."

Sponsor "*Pish tosh, none have proven true o'er the years,
But they waggle on tongues and wiggle in ears.
Her blood is not a poison to the world at large,
Nor is it a potion in a talisman to charge.
Tis but a cleansing of her birthing skill
A monthly preparation, if you will.*"

Male "*'Tis the scourge of Eve, it is, the bible says it's so,
For leading Adam into sin, and causing them to go
From the heavenly garden where the Lord emplanted them,
And then the Lord did both of them condemn.*"

Woman "*Say you a woman's evil when she bleeds?
Have you not prayed for it indeed?
From time to time, when babes weren't wanted,
Your happiness at bleeding time you've flaunted.
Now I see your feelings truly,
Here are mine, delivered cooly.
I will join my sisters of the blood
And welcome in the child, the bud.*"

She enters the moon hut.

The Male slumps, beaten and withdraws to the side.

Child "*Are any of these things he says of truth?
Is this the treasure that ends my youth?*"

Priestess "*Oh daughter, have no fear of these old tales,
These and many more you'll hear, in wails.
But truth be told, a time for celebration is here,
Keep your eye on me and have no earthly fear.*"

Sponsor "*Walk among the rose's petals scattered there,*

    Pointing to the petals
>*Follow them to find the Moon Shelter where*
>*You will join with others who have bled before,*
>*And welcome you to Maidenhood's door."*

Child   (Carefully walking, slowly)
>*"Step by step I travel forth, treading on the red, red rose,*
>*My childhood now will end, transpose."*

As the Child nears the shelter, the Priestess draws a crescent moon on her brow with bright red lipstick.

Sponsor *"She marks you now with a red, red moon,*
>*For now you join Her blest commune.*
>*This mark will fade with passing time,*
>*Yet you will always be a Woman sublime."*

The Sponsor marks the Child's dress with a large crescent moon on both front and back, using a permanent marker, while the Child holds the fabric taut.

Maiden 1 *"And Woman marks your childish dress with red*
>*To make a lovely Goddess gown instead."*

Maiden 2 *"This is a time of inner knowing,*
>*While the outer you keeps growing."*

Maiden 1 *"Your dreams will guide you across the threshold,*
>*And we will strengthen and uphold."*

Maiden 2 *"Cross the threshold gaily, come into Maidenhood,*
>*Join us who bear life within, for all and good."*

Woman   *"Men will fear your fertile power,*
They would envy and deflower.
Let them not deter your passing
Join the women here amassing."

Maiden 1 *"What happens on this special day*
Will stay with you through work and play."

Maiden 2 *"You are changing every moment, becoming more*
Reforming inside-out, better than you were before."

Woman   *"All these changes have begun*
Let us live in unison."

Sponsor *"Thirteen moons rise in every year,*
Thirteen times your body makes it clear
That Goddess dwells within you there"

Child   (Stepping into the shelter)
"I am excited, fearful too, to bear
The burden of approaching woman-ness."

The two Maidens approach the child and hug her in welcome.

Priestess *"Then let us soothe you with our love, no less.*
And bless you with the elements of all creation,
Listen, dear one, to our invocation."

Sponsor (Brushing the child's brow with a red feather)
"May the element of air bring ideas and tender thoughts,
Dreams, imaginings and whatnots."

Woman (Circling the child with a lighted red candle)

> "May the element of fire fuel your passions
> And make you sensual, sensitive, in your fashions."

Sponsor (Sprinkling water on the child from a seashell)
> "May the element of water flow in your intuition,
> And guide you through this new transition."

Woman (Placing the child's hand in a red clay bowl)
> "May the element of earth find a home within you,
> Enabling your fertility in all you seek to do."

Priestess (Motioning with her hand toward the child)
> "May the element of spirit give you joy each day you live,
> Breathing life into all the love you give."

The white curtains are removed and the red curtains now drop down.

Sponsor "I am a daughter; I am a sister; I am a mother;
> I am a woman; I am goddess; I am like no other."

Woman "Now begins your monthly resurrection
> Into fertile liveliness; it has begun."

Sponsor "You are a daughter; you are a sister; you are a goddess;
> You are a woman, you are she whom we bless."

Maiden 1 brings forth honey

Priest "Taste now the sweetness of life as you knew it;
> Know that the sweetness of life remains through it."

Places a drop of honey on the child's tongue

Maiden 2 brings forth salt

Priest   *"Taste now the bitterness that comes with living,*
Know that you'll manage it with thanksgiving."

Places a pinch of salt on the child's tongue

Priestess *"Now eat the red food and swallow the red drink*
Be one with us now, the red is the link."

Maiden 1 and the Woman bring forth a dish of strawberries and a goblet of red drink.

Sponsor (Feeding the child a strawberry)
"May you never hunger, save for liberation
From all that binds you from emancipation."

The others partake of the strawberries as well.

Woman (Serving the child the goblet)
"May you never thirst, save for knowledge
And may you always have that privilege."

The others partake of the goblet as well.

Male   *"Now I see the truth behind the fables*
Woman is a blessing, nevermind the labels.
Let your power surge and fill the earth,
Know your certain power and your worth."

Celebratory music begins to play. All begin to dance about..

Child   *"Let me dance in my freedom, and celebrate life,*
Dance with me sisters, and throw away strife.
I was a child and now am a maiden,

My childish ways now they are fadin'."

Shadowland Rituals

Rituals for dying and for remembering

These rituals were written to be followed for my own death and memorial, and I'm happy to share them with you.

A ritual preparation of the deceased

The first ritual deals with the body of the deceased, and pre-supposes that you have been able to confer with the undertaker in order to have some private time with the body before processing. Whether the body is to be embalmed/buried or cremated, some portion of these small rituals can be incorporated into your process.

It is recommended that this entire ritual be accomplished in relative silence. Speak only when words are necessary for communication. Music may be played softly, if you wish. It is also recommended that you do not attempt this ritual on your own, but gather as many like-minded folk as you can to assist you.

You will need water, herbs of your choice for the washing, a talisman of the psychopomp the deceased most admired, a sprig of fresh basil, a new besom or broom, scissors. Recipes to create the Lustration or Bathing washes can be found in the Appendix. You might also have the opportunity to dress the deceased, in which case you must bring the garments in which s/he has chosen to journey.

You will find a list of psychopomps and their most common talismans at the end of this ritual.

No circle need be cast, as the presence of the deceased sanctifies the space sufficiently for this ritual.

One of the first rituals performed at birth is that of washing the body. As such, it is appropriate that one of the last rituals also be washing the body. In times past, the body was prepared by the next of kin, probably at home, in private, or with the assistance of family and friends. Washing the body is not usually permitted by the authorities in today's modern world, but they will most likely allow the bathing of the deceased's hands. In the case of cremation, all jewelry should be removed before that procedure takes place. This would be an auspicious time for the hand bathing.

If you are fortunate enough to have been granted permission to fully bathe the deceased, you will also be able to dress her or him in the garments chosen for the journey into the Shadowlands. It is hoped that the deceased has made these choices known to the community before passing, perhaps in a will. Should the deceased have chosen to enter the Shadowlands skyclad, you might choose to lay an altar cloth across the more private areas for the viewing, if there is to be one, in the event that non-pagans will be present.

At any rate, the deceased's last wishes should be made known to the authorities and followed as closely as possible. If you are dealing with an undertaker who balks at following those wishes, be as firm as you need to be to get your way in this matter, out of respect for the loved one.

When the washing is completed and the loved one is dressed for the journey, you may place the psychopomp talisman on or near the body. Be sure that the talisman is one that will degrade as the body degrades, perhaps made of paper. You could have it on a chain or ribbon around the neck, or entwined through the fingers, but be certain that it will not be left behind when the body is moved from one place to another.

Clip a lock of the loved one's hair, for the family who will continue to reside in the home she or he lived in. That lock of hair is to be nailed on the lintel (crossbeam) over the main entrance to the home, to carry on prosperity and protection.

At the deceased's home, a new, unused besom or broom should be used to sweep the entire house (or all the parts in which the deceased may have spent time), and the debris collected should either be removed to outside the home or should be burned. If there is a concern that the deceased might return in spirit and cause problems, the broom should also be burned. However, if the spirit of the deceased is to be welcomed in the home, the broom can be used for summoning her or him for future visitations.

Finally, lay a sprig of fresh basil upon the deceased's bare chest, to ensure a safe journey into the Shadowlands. The body is now ready for viewing, for cremation or both.

A ritual memorial service

The body of the deceased is not present for this ritual, therefore it may be held some days or weeks after the actual funeral services. This is an opportunity for the loved one's family and friends (both pagan and non-pagan) to remember her or him in a more relaxed atmosphere. Each guest will have been informed that they could bring a small amount of an herb they have chosen that will relieve grief.

You will need white scented candles, a white altar, and enough white flowers (each in a floral tube) to distribute one to all guests. You will also need a pitcher and blessed water for lustration along with towels, talismans or mementoes of the deceased, small containers of the deceased's ashes (if they are to be distributed among the guests), bread and wine along with cups or a chalice for drinking, scented oils in place of incense (using the same scent as in the candles), a cauldron in which burning will take place and which is standing upon bricks or tiles, a small drawstring bag, a burning mixture of 3 parts rubbing alcohol and 2 parts Epsom salts, and a means of starting the flame. You might also wish to incorporate music that was enjoyed by the deceased, or will be appreciated by the family. If you would rather, you might choose to have drums in place of the music. If you are able, you might want to provide a towel for each guest, which has been in some way identified with the deceased's name and dates of birth and death, as a keepsake. These can be ordered from wedding or party suppliers.

The room or area, if outdoors, should be 'decorated' with things that evoke memories of the deceased. If s/he was a writer, her or his books can be displayed; if an artist, her or his works; if a tarot reader, cards could be enlarged and displayed, etc. Enlargements of photographs of the deceased should also be employed.

No circle will be cast, per se, but the entire area will be blessed and sanctified before the guests arrive. The music or drums should be playing, and the candles burning as they arrive for the service. Each guest is invited to ceremoniously wash their hands in the blessed water as they enter the memorial area.

The guests are invited to place in the cauldron the herbs they have brought to embrace the deceased's family in their grief. When all have done this, the herbs are stirred to blend completely. A small amount of this mixture is placed in the small drawstring bag, to be given to the family, who is present. The remaining herbal mixture will be burned with the burning mixture, at whatever point in the service you feel is appropriate.

The placement and blending of the herbs is followed by the memorial phase. A talisman of the loved one is passed from guest to guest, and now each guest is invited to tell a story about the deceased, or relate a memory they will always revere. Time should be allowed for each guest to say all s/he wishes to impart, before passing the talisman to the next person. When the memorial phase is completed, you might choose to burn the blended herbs.

Bread and wine are now blessed ceremoniously by a Priestess or Priest, and shared by all the guests, using separate cups if there are a large amount of guests, or a single chalice if it is a small gathering.

If the ashes are to be distributed among the guests, this is the time to do so. If not, the music may continue until the family has determined the ritual is ended.

Handfasting

A ritual of joining

You will need a small loaf of sweet bread that the bride and groom alone will share, water and a chalice that the bride and groom will share, a wand to hold both rings that will be exchanged during the ritual, the couple's hand-written vows upon a parchment scroll from which they are permitted to read, ribbons in two colors (one color for the bride and another for the groom) to be used for the binding, a new broom or besom. You will also need stakes and ribbon with which to scribe the circle, leaving a gateway unbound.

You might also want a nuptial tent for the purpose of changing clothes, preparing for the ritual, and for general privacy. This would be recommended if the entire event were to be held at an outdoor location, away from the homes of either the bride or the groom.

It will be noted that, in this ritual, the bride is permitted a maiden to accompany her, while the groom has a warrior. These positions are akin to the non-pagan maid of honor and best man. Also the couple's parents are to be involved if at all possible, and their mothers will take an active part in the ceremony. If the actual parents are not willing to participate, a stand-in for each mother and each father may be appointed by the couple.

The couple is dressed in ornate, hand-made robes, wearing ritual jewelry. Whilst this is taking place, the mothers sprinkle their respective offspring who about to be handfasted with a mixture of salt, grain and tiny golden coins (made of paper, like confetti). As they do this, they utter:

> *"May your joining last for many years, with health, happiness and prosperity."*

The couple and their parents are led by a long procession of guests to the place of the handfasting. The elders lead with the couple, followed by musicians and drummers, then the guests, bearing breads and the other items required for the ritual.

The guests take their places within the temple and the bride and groom stand together before the altar. The Priest explains to all present, in his own words, the meaning of a handfasting, explaining that it is a long-lasting commitment where each party places the welfare and happiness of her or his lover before her or his own.

The Priestess recognizes their intention with these words:

> *"You have come here today to gather with family and friends, within the sacred circle and to stand before your ancestors and in the presence of the Goddess and God, to beseech Them to make of you One, as They are one, and to bestow upon you Their blessing of everlasting love and devotion, through the sacred rite of handfasting."*

To the bride:

> *Do you, before all witnesses present, declare that it is your wish to be formally joined to your beloved?*
>
> *Is it your intention to be bound to this man through vows of devotion and commitment?"*

To the groom:

> *Do you, before all witnesses present, declare that it is your wish to be formally joined to your beloved?*
>
> *Is it your intention to be bound to this woman through vows of devotion and commitment?"*

Next the Priest will ask if anyone present knows any reason why this handfasting should not be celebrated and if anyone objects, saying:

> *"Does anyone say nay to this union? "*

If no objection is forthcoming, the parents of the couple ask for blessings on their children union, asking that it be happy, prosperous and fruitful, the bride's parents first, followed by the groom's parents.

The Priestess asks:

> *"Who stands in support of this woman?"*

The bride's maiden responds.

> *"Who stands in support of the man?"*

The groom's warrior responds.

The Priest asks the couple four questions:

> *"What is it that you ask of the Element of Earth?"*

The response is *"Dependability."*

> *"What is it that you ask of the Element of Water?"*

The response is *"Love."*

"What is it that you ask of the Element of Air?"

The response is *"Consideration."*

"What is it that you ask of the Element of Fire?"

The response is *"Passion."*

The couple now pledges their vows of loyalty, honor, love and conjugal commitment to one another. These will have been self-written and can be read from parchment scrolls upon which the vows have been printed. These scrolls will be used once more in this ritual, at the end of the handfasting. The vows should end with the statement, *"I swear this before all Gods and men!"*

The rings that will be exchanged, and have been placed on the wand, are brought to the couple by the Priestess, who holds the wand in front of them, as each takes hold of an end of the wand, and says:

> *"These rings are tokens of your love for one another, and as you exchange them, so do you offer the gift of mutual respect, which is essential to a lasting relationship."*

To the bride:

> *"Repeat after me...*
> *I, (bride), in the name of the Lady and the Lord which dwells within, and with the love in my heart, take you, (groom), to be my husband and beloved partner. I promise that I will honor our union with love, consideration, respect and support, and I commit myself to work together with you, and to grow with you, through any challenges that lie before*

us."

To the groom:

> *"Repeat after me...*
> *I, (groom), in the name of the Lady and the Lord which dwells within, and with the love in my heart, take you, (bride), to be my husband and beloved partner. I promise that I will honor our union with love, consideration, respect and support, and I commit myself to work together with you, and to grow with you, through any challenges that lie before us."*

The rings are placed upon the couple's hands. The ringed hands are then placed one atop the other, the groom's on top of the bride's. The Priest places his hand atop their hands, saying:

> *"Above you the stars, below you the stones.*
> *Like a star, let your love be constant;*
> *Like a stone, let your love be firm.*
> *Have patience with each other,*
> *freely give your affection and warmth to each other,*
> *for the Goddess and the God are with you,*
> *now and forever."*

The Priestess now asks the couple to present their hands, palms up, to each other, hers atop his, and to face each other, as she says to the groom:

> *"These are the loving hands of your partner, as she pledges her commitment to you all the days of her life. These are the supporting hands that will hold you close as you struggle through difficult times. They are the comforting hands that will console you when your need is great. They are the hands that*

will passionately love you and cherish you through the years, for a lifetime of happiness."

The couple now changes the position of the hands, still palms up, but now his atop hers, as the Priestess speaks to the bride:

"These are the loving hands of your partner, as he promises his commitment to you all the days of his life. These are the strong hands that will passionately love you and cherish you through the years, for a lifetime of happiness. They are the hands that will wipe tears from your eyes, tears of sorrow and tears of joy. They are the hands that comfort you in illness and hold you when fear or grief assail you."

The Priestess places her own hands atop theirs, saying:

"Goddess and God, bless these hands before You this day. May they always be held by one another. Give them the strength to hold on during any storms of stress or darkness of disillusionment. Keep them tender and gentle as they nurture each other in their love. Help these hands to continue building a relationship founded in Your grace, devoted to You. May (bride) and (groom) see their hands as healers, protectors, shelters and guides."

The Priest comes forward with the binding ribbons, and loosely places them across and around the couple's joined, ringed hands, criss-crossing the hands three times, saying:

"The handfasting ribbons, binding the lovers' hand together, represents their sincere and hopeful intention to make an indissoluble union. The ties are comprised of the bride's ribbon and the groom's ribbon, each of which represents the good things

> *that each brings to share in this union."*

To the couple:

> *"Raise your bound hands together, so that all may witness your union."*

They raise their hands and the Priest intones:

> *"Made to measure, wrought to bind, witness now these lives entwined."*

The Priestess and Priest now collect the water and bread, blessing each in turn, according to your usual practice. The chalice of water is handed, without partaking, to the bride's mother, who now hands it to the couple.

> *"I bid you share water, the blood of Sacred Mother and Goddess. Water is life. Water binds us and all living things within the sanctity of Her body. May you never thirst."*

The groom's mother now hands the couple a piece of sweet bread.

> *"I bid you share bread, the bread of life, created from the blessings of the Sacred Mother and Goddess and the energies within Her holy body. May you never hunger."*

The bride and groom share a sip of water and bread and a kiss to seal their vows.

The Priestess now declares the union solemnized:

> *"I hereby declare that (bride) and (groom) have been formally handfasted before the ancient Gods,*

their ancestors, friends and family."

In the meantime, the Priestess has placed the broom across the gateway of the circle. The couple's hands are still bound, symbolizing their pledge of faithfulness. They may now leave the inner circle, but must jump the broom in the process. They are instructed by the Priest:

"The broom is a threshold, and you must jump over it to begin this new journey in your lives, which are now vitally connected to each other. Take this leap of faith into your relationship, showing your dedication to working together through whatever comes your way.
May all here present now welcome this new union into the community, the union of (bride)and (groom)."

Now the reception begins, with feasting, dancing, tossing the bride's bouquet, grabbing the broom* and any other festivities the couple wants included in their party. The first slice of the wedding cake will be laid upon the house altar of their new abode, as an offering to the Gods. As they leave the reception area, the couple is given the parchment scroll of their vows, which they now sign and retain for their lifetime.

---

* An old custom calls for the groom to hold the broom parallel to the floor on one side of the reception room, with all unmarried men on the other side of the room. At a signal, the men will race across the room, where the first to grasp the handle of the broom will be the next to marry. This is an appropriate opposite to the tossing of the bride's bouquet.

Handfasting, II

A short, personal ceremony

Italian wedding customs are among the oldest in the world, dating back to ancient Roman ceremonies. The Roman goddess Juno, guardian of marriage, home and childbirth, made June the most popular month for weddings. Roman brides wore veils to disguise her from evil spirits, who would be jealous of her happiness and try to corrupt her. She carried a bouquet of herbs that represent fidelity and fertility, as well as protecting her from those same evil spirits. The bride's maidens and the groom's men dressed similarly to the principals in order to confuse those spirits, who might attempt to carry away the happy couple.

An Italian wedding begins long before the wedding day, but I won't distract you with a long narrative. Our reportage will begin with the day before the wedding. That's usually when the couple has a rehearsal of the ceremony, followed by a dinner with the wedding party. Italian brides usually wear green at the rehearsal dinner. Green represents the abundance that will follow the couple throughout their marriage. In addition, Italian brides don't wear "something blue", they wear something green on their wedding day, for luck. Italian grooms usually carry a piece of iron ore in a pocket to keep the evil eye (*malocchio*) away from the ceremony.

The bride should not try on her entire outfit even once, before the actual ceremony. Even when she is fully garbed and ready to leave for the place of the celebration, and takes one last look in a mirror to check her appearance (this is good luck), she should still have at least one piece of her ensemble not in place as yet. Perhaps a glove, if she will wear them. Or her shoes.

Our ceremony will take place in a circular area, but not in a traditional pagan circle. An open area must be left for the wedding party to enter and leave, and is not closed during the ceremony. If the ceremony is to be outside, perhaps a small pavilion can be erected for the bride's privacy and preparation, some distance from the circle. Another pavilion can be placed in an opposite direction from the bride's, for the groom's preparation. On the altar, will be placed a bowl of blessed salt, into which the rings have been placed, for cleansing. The rings can be visible for size within the salt. Also on the altar is a garland of leaves and herbs and flowers which will be used to bind the couple. Two scrolls are also there, each containing the vows agreed upon by the couple, which will be read by them during the ceremony. A chalice of wine and a loaf of bread are also on the altar. During the ceremony, a decorated besom is placed at the entrance of the circle.

The bride will be accompanied by a sponsor (which can be a relative or a close friend) in addition to her maidens. The elder females of the group will also accompany her journey from the place where she has dressed to the place of ceremony, paying close attention to everything she does and says.

The groom will be accompanied by a sponsor (which can be a relative or a close friend) in addition to his men. The elder males of the group will also accompany him, following the same instructions as the women accompanying the bride.

As the ceremony is about to begin, the groom and his men walk from their pavilion, hoping to see the good omens mentioned below. If the groom picks up the broom, he will be a helpful husband, and if he comforts the child, he will be a good father. He stands at the opening of the circle, holding the bride's bouquet, to await her. Traditionally, the groom's men, standing with him, tease the groom as he waits, suggesting that she may have changed her mind, gotten lost, or even forgot.

The bride walks from her pavilion to the circle, behind the maidens, and finds there are several items in the pathway, essentially blocking her passage. These items are a broom (not a besom), a child who might be crying or upset in some way, toads, spiders, and black cats. The elder women take note of what she does when she encounters these obstacles. If she picks up the broom, even just to move it, she will keep a clean house. If she stops to assist the child, she will be a good mother. The other items are simply good luck objects placed in her path, so that she will see them.

When the bride reaches the groom, and takes her bouquet, he turns and accompanies her to the altar, as his men have done as the maidens arrived.

As this is a handfasting, the couple will join each other, and no other principal need be involved. However, if the couple so desires, a priestess and priest may officiate the entire ceremony. The remainder of this narrative will presume the couple is joining themselves, with the aid of their wedding party. If you have chosen to utilize a priestess and priest, you may divide the tasks between them, instead of permitting the wedding party to perform them.

The groom's best man asks the groom, aloud, *"Are you ready to embark on this journey with this woman?"* The groom will answer, *"I am."*

The bride's first maid asks the bride, aloud, *"Are you prepared to venture on this journey with this man?"* The bride will answer, *"I am."*

The groom's man will hold the scroll upon which is written the groom's vows, which the groom will read, in such a way that all guests can hear him clearly.

The bride's maiden will hold the scroll upon which is written the bride's vows, which the bride will read, in such a way that all guests can hear her clearly.

From the bowl of salt on the altar, the bride's maid takes the groom's ring, and hands it to the bride, who places it upon her own finger, then on his finger, saying, *"Behold, you are consecrated to me with this ring, and all that I am not will be filled by you, from now."* The groom's best man takes the bride's ring from the salt and hands it to the groom, who places it upon his own finger, and then on hers, making the same statement.

The bride's maidens and the groom's men now take up the garland from the altar and with it, they bind together the wrists of the couple, saying, *"As the sweetness of these flowers, and the strength of these stems connect you to each other, so your life from now will be sweet and strong, and you will be bound to each other in love and fidelity."*

The groom takes the chalice of wine and holds it up so that everyone can see it, saying, *"I call upon the Gods of our ancestors to bless this wine, as they bless our union."* He then offers the first drink to the bride, saying, *"May we never thirst."* He drinks after her, and offers the cup to the maidens and then the groom's men.

The bride takes the bread and holds it up so that everyone can see it, saying, *"I call upon the Goddesses of our ancestors to bless this bread, as they bless our union."* She then offers the first bite to the groom, saying, *"May we never hunger."* She eats after him, offering the bread to the maidens and then the groom's men.

The bride and groom now turn away from the altar, and, still bound by the garland, they approach the besom, which now lays across the opening of the circle. Hand in hand, they jump (or step) over the besom. This act seals the union.

Now the festivities can begin, with dancing, feasting and general mayhem!

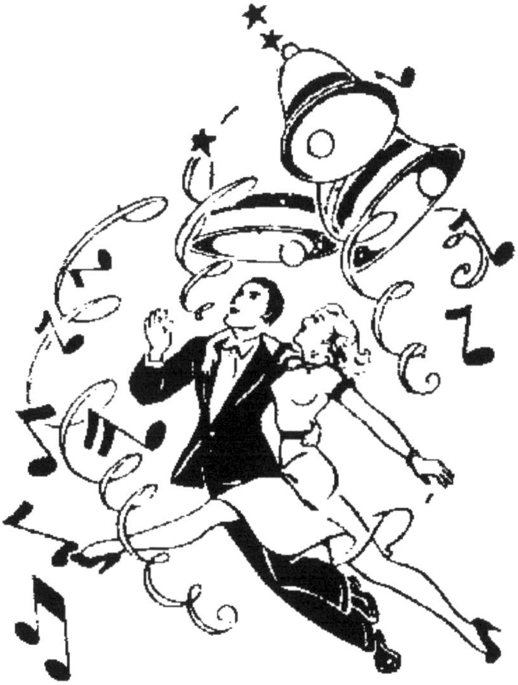

Beltane Handfasting

This ritual was performed in 1995

The circle is drawn at either 9' or 18', whichever the assemblage demands. Within that circle is outlined a 5-pointed star, with small celebratory "altars" at each of the points. A Maypole stands in the center. If it makes you comfortable, you may align your altars with the several directions, but this is an elemental circle, and directions are not required. The Spirit altar will be the main one, and will sit at the point desired by the couple. All other altars are drawn from there. The Spirit altar contains the bridal Besom, a place for the couple to sit, seating also for the HP and HPS, mirrors, tokens of a nature that signifies Spirit to the couple, a bell, and symbols of the God and Goddess, in addition to the marriage certificate, the binding cord an whatever equipment is necessary for the blooding. This is the altar of Immortality.

The Air altar houses many flowers of white color, pinwheels, fans and feathers. A wind chime would also be appropriate at this altar of Beauty.

The Fire altar has red or orange flowers, a charcoal brazier, candles in glass, metal tools or objects, rattles and the

Lover's Candle, as befits the altar of Passion.

The Water altar contains blue flowers, sea shells, a bowl of goldfish, flutes, and wine. This is the altar of Poetry.

The Earth altar may have green plants without flowers, stones, sand, a pentacle, a geode, drums and bread. This is the altar of Power.

The circle is marked around the perimeter by plain besoms, stuck firmly into the earth, brush up. The participants enter the circle directly opposite the main altar.

Anointing/Smudging

> Welcome, my sister (brother), enter in
> The lovers' feast is about to begin
> Enter this haven in perfect trust
> And perfect love, as you must.

The HPS turns the circle:

> Cauldron of changes, feather on the bone,

> Ark of eternity, hole in the stone,
> We are the old ones, we are the new ones,
> Wiser than before, we are the same ones.

The HP turns the circle:

> Water shapes us, Fire transforms us
> Earth heals us, Air moves us
> And the balance of the wheel goes round
> And the balance of the wheel goes round

The HPS now calls the participating couple who will invoke, and hands them the bridal besom for the purpose:

> From the sea entire,
> From the beacon fi re,
> From the earthen stone,
> From the sky, wind blown,
> Call the powerful forces,
> Cause the elements to enter here
> Each from their primal sources
> Let their influence appear!

Holding the besom aloft, at the Water altar, a Priest invokes:

> Sail to us and join this bond
> Liquid love from out beyond
> Steer our course, make it true
> All our song is sung to you.

A PS then chants with her back to the Water altar:

> Take a raindrop, hold it here
> Add a sparkling human tear,
> And a drop of dew, morning-kissed
> Then a touch of mountain mist.
> Warm them gently, these silvery sips,
> Lift this nectar to your lips
> And drink of immortality

So mote it be.

At the Fire altar, a PS holds the besom aloft and invokes:
> Warmly we welcome the flame of passion
> To join this blessing of purest union
> All the fi re of our bright blessing
> Calls you to our circle stressing.

A P then chants with his hack to the Fire altar:
> Rise! Beloved flame of dawn
> Ignite the sky. Waken Oberon.
> Revive us with compassion.
> Excite the life within our passion
> Blessed dragon of the ages
> Teach us through your sacred sages
> Kindle our intensity
> So mote it be.

Again, a P holds the besom aloft, this time at the Air altar, and invokes:

> Soar to us on measured wing
> Bring to us a truth to sing
> Zephyrs kiss this sacred space
> Marked here by measured pace

And a PS chants with her hack to the Air altar:
> On wings of air the magic flies
> We sense an atmosphere of sighs
> The breath of goddess we have found
> And here the magic will abound
> We look upon the sky. We see
> And sing, So mote it be.

Once more, a Priestess holds the besom aloft, now at the Earth altar, and invokes:

> Sow our future in our present

> In Mother's earth so warm and pleasant
> Earthen creatures take delight here
> Join us in our work sincere.

And a Priest chants with his back to the Earth altar:

> She the nurturing mother now revealed
> We the caretakers of her loving field
> The source is lush, green, and supreme
> A place where pagan children dream
> We dance upon her, within her, for her
> We dance and her blessings conjure
> We are her earthborn colony
> So mote it be.

At the Spirit altar, a Priest and Priestess hold the besom together, and they speak the invocation together:

> In this place of wondrous delight
> Of formless universe and might
> Our spirits soar as we would hear
> Unspoken words to calm all fear
> The cauldron holds the echo of our song
> The circle marks the place where we belong
> Sacred Spirit, keep us free
> As we will, so mote it be.

The besom is carried, deosil, to the part of the circle where the bridal couple will enter, and is there handed to the HPS.

The HP cuts a gateway for the entrance, and holding the besom in front of her, the HPS calls:

> I call upon the lovers. If you are ready and do so desire
> A sacred binding union, in the presence of this choir
> Come you now to the portal
> Be admitted, oh mortal.

The lovers enter, and anoint each other, the groom upon the bride's forehead, and the bride upon the groom's heart:

> I offer you
> My body
> My blood
> My breath
> My passion
> My spirit
> For all the days we live together.

(While speaking these words, draw a pentagram on the partner, with the last line speaking the containing circle.)

The HPS introduces the lovers to the assembly, as the HP closes the gateway:

> Through the gateway we allow
> Come the lovers now
> Come they to be joined as one
> Wish them well as best you can
> This woman... and this man.

The lovers take up their place in front of the Spirit altar, with the HPS and HP on either side of the altar. The guests travel round the circle with flowers (or flower petals), which they sprinkle upon the ground, as they speak their good wishes to the lovers when they approach:

(Following are a few example of the manner of good wishes)

> Let your love be as flowers to the earth.
>> Let it create an ever growing circle that spreads love and joy over the earth.
>
> May you exist within a circle of love.
> May your union be a thing of beauty.
> May your love dance in the eternal circles of time,
>> with the dance of the earth, with the sacredness of life.

The HPS pronounces the circle cast:
>   The circle is cast
>   The spell is made fast
>   There is yang, there is yin
>   The magic is here, so let it begin!

A female guest draws the groom's hood up over his head, saying:
>   This is a symbol of defense. You wear it to show your separateness.

A male guest places a veil over the bride's head, saying:
>   This is a shield of influence. You cover yourself in differentness.

A male guest, at the Water altar, speaks to the bride:
>   You are the water, my sister
>   You are sensitive and brave
>   The very vessel of love
>   We welcome the water in you
>   This is the beginning

The bride then turns to the groom and vows:
>   I give you this (symbol), a part of me, for I am the water.
>   This is the element of integration, and I give it to you as a sign of our togethering.

A female guest, at the Fire altar, speaks to the groom:
>   You are the fire, my brother
>   You are vigorous and true
>   The bright passion of power
>   We welcome the fire in you
>   And so it continues.

The groom turns to the bride and vows:

> I give you this (symbol), that represents me, for I am the fire.
> This is the element of beginnings, and I give it to you as a symbol of our new life together.

A male guest, at the Earth altar, speaks to the bride:

> You are the earth, my sister
> You are centered, enduring
> The mysterious essence of life
> We welcome the earth in you
> And so the cycle goes.

The bride turns to the groom, vowing:

> I give you this (symbol), which is me, for I am the earth.
> This is the element of completion, and I give it to you as a symbol of our wholeness.

A female guest, at the Air altar, speaks to the groom:

> You are the air, my brother
> You are the inspiration
> The clear breath of freedom
> We welcome the air in you
> And tis nearly done.

The groom turns to the bride, vowing:

> I give you this (symbol), which is a symbol of myself: for I am the air.
> This is the element of merging, and I give it to you as a sign of our union.

At the Spirit altar, the HP places the lovers hands together, saying:

> Together you are the spirit, beloveds
> You are magic, balance and unity
> You are all that is
> We welcome the loving spirit in you

And now it is drawn.

The bride removes the groom's hood from his head, saying:

> I take from you this symbol of defense, which is a part of you, for you are the spirit.

The groom removes the bride's veil, saying:
> This is the element of growth and I take this emblem from you as a sign of our trust in each other.

The lovers kiss. Then the HPS asks the gathering:
> Be there one against this union
> Speak you now before tis done
> Before we take up our communion
> Before we dance around the sun.

A moment is waited in silence, and if there is no reply, the HPS calls:

> Take you now a colored strand
> Hearken to the human band
> Dance the spiral, thrum the drum
> Out you go and in you come.
> Round and round, bring in the May
> Knowing spring is nature's foreplay
> Dance you while the sun does shine
> Dance and then we drink May wine.

The HP loosens the Maypole ribbons, the music rises and the dance ensues. You may allow the dance to continue as long as you wish, but be aware that there is still much to do. When the Maypole dance is ended, if it is feasible, remove the pole from the center of the circle, cutting a gateway through which can be taken out of the circle entirely. If this is not feasible, the following vow can be made just to one side of the pole.

In the center of the circle, the lovers face each other, she facing west and he facing east. The bride begins a salutatory great rite, with her hands over the groom's eyes:

> Blessed be your eyes, that see the loveliness within me.

The groom places his hands on the bride's ears:
> Blessed be your ears, that listen for the love in my words.

The bride places her hand upon his mouth:
> Blessed be your lips, that speak of love to me.

The groom holds both her arms:
> Blessed be your arms, that willingly embrace me.

The bride places her hands upon his shoulders:
> Blessed be your shoulders that offer understanding and comfort

The groom places his hands upon her hands:
> Blessed be your hands, that touch me lovingly.

The bride places her hand over his heart:
> Blessed be your heart, that sings at my touch.

The groom places his hand over her genitals:
> Blessed be your charm, the gateway to rapture.

The bride places her hand over his genitals:
> Blessed be your power, the key to ecstacy.

The groom touches her legs:
> Blessed be your legs, that carry you to me.

The bride touches his feet:
> Blessed be your feet. that take you on love's

journey.

The bride and groom now speak to the gathered company:

We are love united. Blessed be!

The lovers kiss a second time, then await the guests' blessing.

Three couples from among the guests rise and each person speaks:

These children of love and light
Have come to share the Beltane rite.
They are united 'neath a sacred sky
Their loving hearts to satisfy.
They submit to blessed power
Here is the place, now is the hour.
They accept the gift entwined
They were two, now one, combined.
They perceive their unison
Let the ritual be done.
Bless them with awareness please
With romance and with memories.

When all this has been spoken, the three couples join hands and rade around the circle, encircling the couple three times. The lovers now walk deosil until they arrive back at the Spirit altar, where they stand facing each other. The groom speaks first:

I would travel this while with you.
Be my guide and I shall be your companion.
I take you in good times and in bad.
I take you as my center, for you are my bliss.

The bride speaks:

I would do the dance of love with you.
Be my partner and I shall be your friend.
I take you to be my consort.
I will keep my love and trust for you all ways.

They kiss a third time, sealing the three vows now spoken. The HP speaks:

> Three times have they now sworn
> To ride the loving unicorn.
> Three times they shared a blessed kiss
> Born of love, invoking benefice.
> Three times will they dance the circle here
> And we will join their wedded cheer.

The HPS walks to the Earth altar and tells the company:

> Now the sacrifice must come
> Bread and wine now will become
> Body, blood of sacredness
> Be seated. Comes the blessedness.

She holds an empty bread basket and the bride and groom stand on either side of the basket. The groom picks up the uncut bread that has been prepared for the sacred feast, and speaks to the bride:

> I am the seed that enters you.

The bride holds up a cutting board upon which the groom places the bread, and speaks to him:

> I am the earth that nurtures you.

The groom cuts the bread, saying:
> I am the blade that mows the wheat.

The bride places the cut bread into the empty basket, saying:

> I am the oven of making complete.

The bride and groom say to each other:

> We are the blessing of bread. So mote it be.

The HPS tells them:

> Eat of this sustenance
> Seed of the earth
> Forming food of the Goddess

They feed each other, then pass the basket round to the guests.

The HP walks to the water altar and holds a large, empty chalice. The groom pours May wine into the chalice, filling it only halfway, and saying:

> I am the sun that ripens the fruit.

(The red wine mentioned here can be a rose, if you prefer, or you could use a Sangria made with juniper berries.)

The bride pours red wine into the chalice, to fill it up, saying:

> I am the fertile soil where it took root.

The groom mixes the two wines with his athame, saying:
> I am the decanter of giving.

The bride adds the merest pinch of salt, saying:
> I am the chalice of living.

The bride and the groom speak to the company, saying:
> We are the blessing of wine. So mote it be.

The HP tells them:
> Drink of this sweetness
> Juices of life
> From the body of the Goddess.

They feed each other, then pass the chalice to each of their guests.

The HPS claps her hands three times, saying:
> By bud and stem, seed and root
> By leaf and flower, vine and fruit
> I command you turn the circle round

> Dancing body to spirit bound.

At this, the bride and groom dance together, deosil, around the circle. Only they dance; the others may sing, chant, whistle, drum or keep rhythm, but they do not dance this time. When the time feels right and the dancing has progressed at least three times around the circle, the HP calls:

> By sun and moon, wind and rain
> By star and planet, blood and brain
> I command your attention here and now
> For the Goddess has heard your loving vow.

(The couple will have decided prior to this time whether theirs is to be a blood ceremony, or one that is symbolic. The equipment for whichever manner will have been placed upon the Spirit altar before the ritual began. For a blood ceremony, sterile prickers (2) will be needed. For a symbolic ceremony, a red marker will suffice, and the Priestess will draw a pentagram on each hand in such a way that when the hands are joined, the pentagrams are against each other.)

At the Spirit altar, the HPS pricks (or draws) the hands of the lovers and places their palms together:

> As you are drawn out each into the other
> So it is drawn unto you, sister, brother.

Their hands are bound by the HP and HPS with a ribbon made of two strands, two colors, and two fibers. The HP pronounces:

> By the power of the Goddess and in the name of
> these her children, you are bound together.

With their hands bound, the lovers walk around the circle while the company chants:

> Hand to hand, hear to heart, spirit to spirit

The HPS blesses the couple as they stand in front of the Spirit altar:

> As above, so below
> As the universe, so the soul
> As without, so within
> Masculine and feminine
> May you know peace in all your days
> And joy in all your nights.

Two guests bring the bridal besom forward and hold it at either end, saying:

> Jump the besom of renown
> Seal the union, wear the crown!

The lovers jump the broom and the HP unbinds their hands. The HPS crowns the groom with an herbal and floral wreath, saying:

> May the Goddess protect your unity!

The HP crowns the bride in the same manner, saying:

> May the Goddess project your destiny!

The HPS cries:

> As I have woven it
> So mote it be!

The bride and groom say:

> So it is! So shall it be!

The HP speaks to the newlywedded couple:

> Share yourselves one more time
> With those who love you well
> Dance the circle all sublime
> Dance until the Goddess Bell

The bride and groom now dance with their guests. Be sure to allot enough time for the bride to dance with each male guest and the HP, and for the groom to dance with each female guest and the HPS. When all have had an opportunity to dance, the HP will ring a bell as a signal to stop. The HP speaks to the couple:

> May you revere each other
> May you honor the Mother

The HPS scribes a pentagram over them as she says:
> In all your many lifetimes
> In the past and yet to come
> You are fastened heart and soul
> As I will it, be it so!

A guest now begins to open the circle:
> Now thank we water and the fire
> The earth and the air, we retire

Another guest speaks:
> The loving spirit that joined us here
> The blessed Goddess we revere

Yet another guest:
> Return to the realms from whence you came
> Blessing the work we've done in your name

And another guest:
> The circle is open, yet unbroken Merry meet, merry part, and merry meet again

Lunar Rituals

All rituals that are performed to honor the moon (lunar rituals) are called esbats. The word 'esbat' comes to us from Old French, *'esbattre'*, which translates 'to frolic joyfully'; which, in turn, comes from the Latin *'ex'*, combined with *'battuere'*, meaning to pound or beat. Within the pagan community, esbat refers to lunar rituals, usually the full moon ritual, yet without the pagan community, the word seems to mean 'a gathering of witches'.

Lunar rituals are performed to focus the energy of the moon to help us to move through the continuing cycle (waxing and waning, fulfilling and freeing, dying and renewing) of the events in our lives. Using that energy allows us to attain the powerful natural energies of the moon's phases by embracing and focusing these energies in ourselves, through the phases of our lives.

The phases of the Moon

New Moon - At the start of the phases, the Moon is invisible, hidden by the light of the Sun. The Moon gradually waxes toward the 1st quarter. and a slender sliver can be seen two to three days after the new moon date, which is the period from three days before the actual New Moon until three days after it, and is generally regarded as a time of minimum energy, linked to the Crone Aspect of the Goddess, and a time for reflection and contemplation. It is a time for change, transformation or the beginning of a new cycle.

First Quarter - The waxing, or growing Moon can now be seen in the United States, in the western skies at early evening. This phase begins from about 4 days after the New Moon, and lasts until three days before the Full Moon. It is a time of development and growth, linked to the Maiden Aspect of the Goddess. Projects should be maturing, building.

Full Moon - At this time, the Sun and Moon are in exact opposition and the moon reflects all of the Sun's light. The Full Moon starts from about three days before the actual Full Moon, and lasts until about three days afterwards. Energy is considered to be at its maximum, and is linked to the Mother Aspect of the Goddess, maturity, creation, psychic abilities and fertility. February is the only month of the year which can have no full moon. The last such February was in 1866. In some Chinese religions, offerings are made to the ancestors on the night of a full moon.

Last Quarter - The final phase of the Moon is a 'mirror image' of the first quarter. This is a quiet time of banishment of negativity. It starts about four days after the Full Moon, and lasts until about four days before the New Moon. Her energy is considered to be growing smaller, and is linked with the Crone Aspect of the Goddess, reversing spells, banishing and releasing, cleansing, purging, and clearing.

Moon Trivia

The time period between a New Moon and the next New Moon is 27.3 days. And did you know that we are able to see only 60% of the Moon's surface from Earth? Even more interesting, is that the Moon is moving away from the Earth, at a rate of 1 ½ inches each year.

Once, people believed the shadowed areas of the Moon were the forests where the Goddess Diana hunted. Some also believed the Moon was a jewel worn by the Goddess and the stars were the decorations on her gown.

Romancing the Moon

A Full Moon Ritual

Prior to the ritual, you must prepare a bowl of Moon Wash as well as a pitcher of Moon Waters to be used in the ritual. These are prepared very simply:

Begin with a clear glass bowl, which you have washed thoroughly. Complete a final rinse of the bowl with either spring water or distilled water, and fill the bowl with the same. Add a piece of Moonstone to the water, and cover the bowl with clear plastic wrap. Set it outside, or in a window where the full Moon will shine upon it all night long. For the pitcher, clean a clear glass jar or pitcher in the same manner, doing a final rinse with spring or distilled water, and fill the pitcher with the same. Add a larger piece of Moonstone to the water, and cover the pitcher with a piece of clear plastic wrap. Set this also outside, or in a Moonlit window. Leave the waters there to charge all night, collecting it in the morning, and covering it quickly with a dark cloth until time for the ritual. This can be done the night before the ritual, since the Moon's power is available three days before and three days after the calendar date and time of the Moon's full phase..

You will also make Moon Cakes for the ritual, and coat them well with Confectioner's Sugar, also called 10X. A recipe for the Moon Cakes, if you require it, can be found in the Appendix. The pitcher of Moon Waters, along with a chalice, should be close by the Moon Cakes.

The altar should be set with a white cloth, two floating candles (one white or silver and one yellow or gold), white or silver and yellow or gold ribbons and as many mirrors as you can find. You will need patchouli incense and a holder. A towel should be placed at the entrance to the sacred circle area, next to the bowl of Moon Wash.

Participants should wear a white garment, which may be covered with a dark cloak for the journey to the circle, but a place to leave the cloak should be provided at the entrance to the sacred circle.

I

n an area where the Moon is fully visible, cast the circle in your usual manner. I suggest the following, if you desire:

At the western point -

"Hail to the Maiden. Come, and bring with You the Goddess' love into our emotions."

At the northern point -

"Hail to the Mother. Come, and bring with You the Goddess' power into our bodies."

At the eastern point -

"Hail to the Crone. Come, and bring with You the Goddess' wisdom into our minds."

At the southern point -

"Hail to the Goddess. Come, and bring Yourself into our spirits."

After the circle has been cast in the names of the Maiden, the Mother and the Crone, the participants may enter the sacred circle. They are invited to take water from the Moon Wash bowl to briefly splash water on their face(s) and hands, and use the towel nearby to dry themselves. This is done in lieu of anointing, therefore, each guest may speak her or his own anointing statement while 'washing'.

When all guests have 'bathed' and have taken their place within the circle, bring the bowl of Moon Wash to the altar, and place two floating candles upon the water, one white (or silver) and one gold (or yellow). Light the Candles, as you call upon the Goddess and God to join the circle:

"Goddess of the Moon, Mistress of Magic and Mystery, come forth and join us here, we pray."

"God of the Sun, Master of Beasts and Power, come forth

and join us here, we pray."

Then all the guests begin to walk deosil around the circle interior, inviting aloud all the lunar Goddesses known to your group. This can be started by the group leader, and others may call out the names of other Goddesses as the leader begins to hesitate. A list of Lunar Goddesses, to refresh your memory, can be found at the end of this ritual narrative. It is most effective if a Lunar Goddess is named at each elemental point of the circle. This procession should continue around the circle at least three times. (More ambulations may be added if more Goddess names are wanted to be called.)

The guests will return to the outer edges of the circle, where each participant will do exactly as the leader does for the next part of the ritual, although each may use her or his own words. Cup your hands and raise them so that the visible full Moon seems to be sitting upon your cupped hands.

"Queen of the Night, Mistress of the Tides, filled with the white milk of divine life, I greet You and invite You to recline here, upon my hands, for I adore You and will uphold You in this world and all others. Hold me in Your arms, as I hold You in my hands.

"Sit upon my hands while You rest from Your labors of creation. Take Your ease here after Your great toil for my benefit. Repose Yourself from the throes of maintaining the life I share on this earth. Hold me in Your arms, as I hold You in my hands."

Give each guest enough time to complete whatever sentiments they wish to express at this time to the Lady Moon. The hands upon which the Moon has rested through this exercise may be kissed and then blown to Her, in remembrance of an ages-old ritual.

A meditation follows, briefly, in which the guests are encouraged to inhale deeply of the Moonlight flooding the sacred circle.

Light the patchouli incense, allowing it to waft over the guests before being placed in its holder.

"The tide-power of the Moon is great, as the Gods are great. We stand before the Goddess in love and adoration. Come fill us with Your presence and be with us. Dance with us and show us the passion You employed to create everything."

After a few moments, let the music begin. This can be recorded music of your choice, or simply drumming. The dancing will be more enjoyable for all, if the group is of mixed gender, but even if it is all female, or all male, the dance should continue. Ritual dance is a unique form of movement. It is performed because through the act of dancing, the participants can communicate ideas and messages that cannot be said in ordinary words. Cultures around the world use rhythmic bodily movement as an integral part of spiritual practice. We dance to demonstrate our devotion and commitment; to invoke the presence of goddesses and gods; to communicate our grievances and receive divine counsel; to attain mystical experience; or to share wisdom within a community.

Without actually pairing off, the dancers should find themselves drawn to each other, yet be unable (or unwilling) to touch each other during the entire dance. This can be accomplished by getting physically close and teasing each other only through the gyrating of hips and shoulders; an interplay between male and female gender, feeling the music. This is a seductive dance, in which you are enacting the Moon's pull upon the waters of the Earth, and Her irresistible power over them and you.

(If you determine that, in your group, it will be necessary to pair off, it might be fun to have each couple dance - together - within the confines of a hula-hoop, still not touching each other.)

If you are performing this ritual alone (and dancing alone), let the outer edge of your sacred circle be the magnetic force that pulls you close, which you can barely resist, but never touch.

During this erotic dance ritual, the females could actually invoke the Lunar Goddess in all Her glory. This, of course, would entice the males, and permit some exciting dancing, with unbelievable power being raised in the process. If you have a spell to be performed at this time, the dance could be quite sufficient to empower the spell. Or, to simply return that energy to the Earth for Her own use.

The dance is to be rather slow, sensual and delicious, not fast and rowdy. I suggest some of Wendy Rule's recordings, or those of Enigma might be appropriate.

When the group's energy is exhausted, and they all prefer to rest, it is time to present the Moon Cakes and Moon Waters for a sacred meal. These should be blessed and shared with the deities as you usually do, and the guests should be made aware that they are drinking Waters that have been specially charged by the Full Moon.

Drawing Down the Crone

A New Moon ritual

Setting up the ritual area

This ritual is meant to stimulate all six senses of the worshiper, while its primary purpose is to draw down the dark moon (the crone). Comfort is most important during this ritual, so the worshipers are to be seated. They may be seated on soft velvet cushions, or on a luxurious length of fake fur. Either of these would satisfy the **sense of touch**.

For the **sense of smell**, surround the circle area with night-blooming plants, or failing that, incense with the refreshing scent of a soft rain.

The **sense of hearing** can be charmed with tinkling bells, a drum or great chimes. Alternatively, worshipers could be told to be still until the sound of the bell, drum or chime has stopped, thereby noticing the absence of sound, which would be spiritually connected to the absence of the moon. Silence is also a sound.

For the **sense of sight**, mirrors can be used in abundance. The altar can be covered in mirrors, or the circle itself can be outlined with small circular mirrors. The altar should shimmer, and for that, use as much silver as you can accumulate, polished and shining. Crystal is also shimmering, when combined with candlelight.

The **sense of taste** will be titillated during the sacred meal portion of the ritual, and you can use a white wine or clear spring water for the beverage and moon cakes sensuously coated with white frosting or confectioner's sugar for the cake. See the end of this section for Moon Cake recipes.

The **sense of self** or spirit is gratified by not only the combination of all these things, but also by the ritual itself, which is written to be romantic, evocative and soothing.

The Ritual Begins

This is a ritual that takes place within another ritual. I have omitted the outer ritual, which each group will have completed beforehand, including casting and dedicating a circle, welcoming any guests into the sacred space and concluding any business that must be done before the 'main event'.

The priestess evokes the Goddess, through her vessel, the moon, in preparation for the Drawing Down:

Return to me, Goddess, and all solitude will end
You are the spirit of my body
You are the life in my universe

Re-member me, Goddess, and we will be new
You are the ring in which I circle
You are the circle in which I pray

Awaken me, Goddess, from this earthly trance
You are the mystery of my quest
You are the dream of my desire

Lay with me, Goddess, upon the fertile earth
You are the lure that beckons me
You are the guide who leads me

Become with me, Goddess, and we will arise
You are my beginning and my end
You are the promise of renewal

Grow with me, Goddess, and we'll be complete
You are the abyss within my hope
You are the hollow inside me

Rise with me, Goddess, illuminating both
You are the jewel in every crown
You are the memory in every thought

Stay with me, Goddess, until the sun is risen
You are the labyrinth

You are every and all.

The priestess speaks to the Crone moon, in her celestial darkness:

Grandmother Moon, be the best part of me
Let my feet be as faithful as your rising and setting
Let my legs be as firm as your phases, one following another
Let my belly be as fertile as your darkness is deep
Let my breast be as comforting as your constant return
Let my heart be as true as your ancient journey
Let my voice be as feminine as you are yourself
Let my mind be as clear as the path on which you lead me.

The priestess now dances, deosil, within the circle, to entertain and please the Crone. The dance must be lively and feminine, delicate and powerful. It should encompass all the phases of a woman's life, from birth, childhood, maidenhood or menarche, the discovery of sexual passion, birthing, mothering, aging, loss, and death. Each priestess is able to show her own creativity in designing this dance.

Some priestesses may choose to execute this dance as Salome's dance of the veils, with each veil representing a time of life, completing the dance skyclad. This is not required, but certainly would add power to the performance.

The Priestess consumes the Moon-infused water, specifically created for this ritual. (A clear glass container of purest spring water is placed outdoors in the evening of the full moon's brightest nights. It must be positioned so that the moon is reflected in the water. This may require moving the container from time to time. Continue to 'collect' the moon in the water as long as you can, before covering the container and bringing it inside for the night. Bring it out again the following evening as the moon rises, and do this for the entire three nights of the full moon and her two following nights. When the container is indoors during the day, be sure to keep it covered with a dark cloth, that none of the moon's power escape. Store the fully-infused moon water in darkness, covered securely, until it is needed at the dark moon.)

The Drawing Down begins:

Just touch me and I will be whole
Let me feel the depth of my soul.

Blow the scent of your wisdom round about
Let me know sense harmony within and without.

Let me inhale the silvery shadow that is your power
And breathe it out to your children at this hour.

Whisper that I might hear the voice of the womb
I'll listen in rapture while your messages loom.

Show me your face, e'en now in the dark
My own face will shine, reflecting the spark.

Savor my longing, the words on my tongue
Are sent for your favor, with passion they're sung.

Now enter me, Goddess, and we will be one
The song has now ended, enchantment's begun.

The priestess now awaits the inspiration of the Crone, seated in the center of the circle. Music can be played *very* softly during this waiting period, so it doesn't interfere with the worshipers' ability to meditate and listen for the Crone's words. Should the priestess have been entered successfully by the Crone, she will feel compelled to speak, and must do so.

When the Crone has spoken, or when enough time has passed and the priestess believes she has not been visited by the Crone this moon, the worshipers will rise, encircling the priestess who now stands within the circle. Each participant recites a quotation, such as:

There are no laurels in life ... just new challenges.

Life's what's important. Home, Family, Birth, Pain and Joy.

Never lose sight of the fact that just being is fun.

You get whatever accomplishment you are willing to declare.

Never let fear keep you from doing a thing you want to do.

Figuring out our gifts in life is part of our journey to becoming enlightened human beings.

This part of the ritual will be led by another priestess other than the one who has officiated so far.

The sacred meal is prepared.

Priestess:

Goddess, bless the food you place before us,
Hear us as we raise our voices in your sacred chorus.
Scented cakes await our hungry spirits,
Round and luscious, they are for our benefit.
Taste with us their sweetened flavors,
Morsels of love to reward your favors.

Crumbs are shared with the earth, and the priestess partakes of the blessed cakes, then distributes them to the worshipers, saying:

May you never hunger.

Priestess:

Goddess, bless the beverage in this chalice,
Taken from the earth with no human malice.

Crisp and cold it beckons our thirst,
Let it delight our sense of smell at first.
Hear it rushing, tumbling in the cup,
Savor it with us as we all do sup.

Droplets are shared with the earth, and the priestess partakes of the blessed beverage, then distributes it to the worshipers, saying:

May you never thirst.

The original priestess returns to begin the closing of the circle, having rested through the sacred meal.

You are the life in my universe
You are the circle in which I pray
You are the mystery of my quest
You are the guide who leads me
You are my beginning and my end
You are the jewel in every crown
You are the memory in every thought
You are the labyrinth
You are every and all.
Beloved Goddess, return now to your realm, taking with you our love and thanks,
Watch us over, night and day, in your fullness, in your darkness.
So mote it be.

At this point the priestess who originally cast the circle continues to close the circle.

APPENDICES

I. Color Chart for Solstice Dancers

White   Purifies, cleanses, spacious

Gray   Calming, elegance, humility, respect, reverence, stability, subtlety

Red   Passionate, loving, alerting, active, courageous, dangerous, energizing, aggressive, bold

Blue   Soothing, calm, cool, communicative, weightless

Dark Blue   Dignified, authoritative, stability

Indigo   Spiritual, intuitive

Light Blue   Ethereal, soft, inspirational, lowers vitality

Green	Restful, calm, balanced, inspirational, generous, sexual
Yellow	Intellectual stimulant, detached, perceptive
Orange	Creative, joyful, lightness, releasing, motion, pleasure
Turquoise	Refreshing, soothing, compassionate, friendly
Violet	Calm body-balanced mind, meditative, magic
Magenta	Spiritually fulfilling, contented, complete, self-respecting, creative
Purple	Sensitive, vibrant, aware, sensuality, spirituality, creativity, ceremonial, enlightened, flamboyant
Rose	Optimism, romantic love, innocence, simplicity
Pink	Tranquilizer, admiration, health, joy, flirtatiousness, innocence
Brown	Comforting, calm, boldness, rusticity, stability, tradition, wholesome, steadfast, dependable

II. May Wines

Non-Alcoholic May Wine

3/4 cup dried woodruff
2 quarts apple cider (or apple juice)
Allow this to macerate for about a week, in a dark place, shaking occasionally, then strain out the herbs.
Add 1 quart ginger ale just before serving.

Traditional May Wine

½ cup dried woodruff
1 bottle dry white wine
Allow this to macerate in a dark place, shaking occasionally, for 2 weeks to 1 month, no longer.
Strain the mixture and add ½ cup superfine sugar. Allow it to dissolve.
Chill until serving time.
Just before serving, add 1 whole bottle sparkling white wine.

Suggested decorations for the May Tree

Have plenty of symbols of fertility, fecundity, sexuality or of spring, for the tree!

(Have enough of each decoration on hand to permit adequate coverage of the tree. These can be hand made by the participants before the ritual, if desired.)

artificial birds and nests
flowers
colorful ribbon bows
rabbits
monkeys
cats
dogs
decorated eggs
pinwheels
rainbows
umbrellas
kites
butterflies
dragonflies
acorns
apples
pomegranates

figs
corn
cornucopia
Earth (the planet)
frogs, toads
grapes
horseshoes
stork
the Moon
pearls
pine cones
spirals
stags
phalluses

Making Floral Garlands and Wreaths

For a Floral Garland...

Use flowers that look fresh for awhile after removing from a water source such as carnations, chrysanthemums, *gypsophilia* or baby's breath, *solidago*, or smaller rose varieties. Fresh flower garlands must be made 24 hours or less before use.

Step 1
Measure the length of the area where the flower garland will be displayed and clear a sufficient space for building the garland and for supplies. All supplies, including flowers and greenery, should be within easy reach. Mark a place on the work bench or table that designates the desired length of the garland.

Step 2
Prepare fresh flowers and greenery by cutting an inch from the bottom of the stems and placing the stem ends in water for 12-24 hours before making the fresh flower garland. This will allow plant material to hydrate before constructing the garland and prevent flowers from wilting prematurely.

Step 3
Place some greenery on the table then add another piece letting it overlap slightly and secure the greenery together with wire, string or thread. Add more greenery, letting it overlap the previous piece, and tie the stems together with wire, string or thread, depending on size and weight of the eventual piece. Choose a side that will not be seen once the flower garland is displayed and make that the side where the stems and wire will be visible. This is the side you will access when making adjustments and attaching the flowers and greenery. Continue overlapping greenery and tying the stems until your reach the desired length of garland. Add all the greenery before adding flowers. The greenery will be your base.

Step 4
Add flowers as needed. If adding different sized flowers, add smaller flowers first. Use string, thread or wire to attach flowers to the greenery by inserting the flowers into the greenery and tying in the area that cannot be seen once the garland is displayed. The flowers should generally point

in the same direction as the greenery. Space larger flowers evenly. Continue until garland is finished.

Step 5
Trim off all excess and visible wire or string and the garland is ready for display.

For a Floral Wreath...

Step 1
Clip the stems off the flowers close to the head of the flower.

Step 2
Cut a length of thread 48 inches long. Thread the needle, doubling the thread and knotting the end.

Step 3
Thread the first flower into the needle, inserting the needle up through the flower from the stem.

Step 4
Continue to string flowers until you have a section 16 to 18 inches long for a woman or 12 to 15 inches for a child.

Step 5
Push the flowers up the string until you have a long tail of thread at either end of the garland. Knot the ends of the thread together, tying the knot close to the flowers.

Step 6
Tie ribbon streamers around the knot to hide it and as decoration for the headdress.

III. Fairy Wine

Makes enough for 8 to 10 humans or swarms of fairies.

3 quarts milk
1/8 cup honey
1 teaspoon vanilla extract
Cinnamon

Warm the milk but do not boil it. Add the honey and vanilla, and stir to melt the honey into the milk completely. Cool this and then chill it. Serve with cinnamon sprinkled on top.

To make only enough for the fairies,
1 ½ cups milk
1 teaspoon honey
1/8 teaspoon vanilla extract
pinch Cinnamon

IV. La Giornata della Dea

Barley Water

Ingredients:
1 cup pearl barley, rinsed
4-6 springs of pennyroyal, tied into a knot
2 quarts spring water (or distilled water)
Zest of 2 lemons (optional)
rock sugar or sugar, to taste

Directions:
1. Place the barley, pennyroyal and water in a pot. Soak for one hour or more.
2. Bring to a boil and simmer for 45 minutes or until the barley is tender. Add in the sugar and bring to a boil.
3. Strain out the barley and pennyroyal. Add the lemon zest.
3. Serve warmed.

V. Abbondanza!

Music Suggestions

If desired, drumming and/or singing may complete the day's feasting. There are many harvest songs that are sung traditionally in the mundane faction, but are not specifically derived from any religious viewpoint, which can be incorporated into this activity. They include:

"We Gather Together to Ask the Lord's Blessing"
"For the Beauty of the Earth, We Thank Thee"
"Bless this House, oh Lord We Pray"
"Shine on Harvest Moon"

Some popular and traditional music that you might wish to include as background music while feasting include:

I can Only Imagine - Mercy Me
Thank God for Kids - Kenney Chesney
Thank God I Found You - Mariah Carey
Thank You Lord - Shaggy (or Bob Marley)
Thank You - Dido
Give Peace A Chance - John Lennon
Travelin' Prayer - Billy Joel
Be Our Guest - Beauty & The Beast
Kind And Generous - Natalie Merchant
Be Thankful - Natalie Cole
Thank You For Loving Me - Bon Jovi
The Thanksgiving song - Adam Sandler
Thank You - Led Zeppelin
Give Thanks & Praise - Bob Marley
A Charlie Brown Thanksgiving - George Winston
Thankful - Kelly Clarkson
What A Wonderful World - Louis Armstrong
I'm Gonna Eat On Thanksgiving Day - Laurie Berkner
American Land - Bruce Springsteen
I've Got Plenty To Be Thankful For - Bing Crosby
Thank You For The Music - ABBA
Eat it - Weird Al Yankovic

I've Got So Much Love To Give - Barry White
Thank You for Being a Friend - Andrew Gold
Wind Beneath My Wings - Bette Midler
Fields of Gold - Sting
Scarborough Fair - Simon & Garfunkel
Red Red Wine - UB40
Harvest Moon - Neil Young
Wind that Shakes the Barley - Solas
Harvest Home - Big Country
The Scythe - Gaia Consort
King Harvest (has Surely Come) - The Band
John Barleycorn - Traffic
Whispering Hope - Jo Stafford (or Pat Boone)

VI. Croning Ritual

Goddess Oil for Anointing:

Make this during a waning moon.

½ teaspoon dried yarrow
½ teaspoon dried basil
1 teaspoon myrrh (beads, not oil)
3 drops essential rose oil
3 drops essential lavender oil
½ cup olive oil

Swirl deosil to mix. Seal and store in a dark place for 7 days. Each day, swirl the container three times deosil and place again in the dark place. Strain through a cloth; do not use a coffee filter. Make the recipe three times, for the magic of three and to have enough for several occasions. You might also wish to give small vials of this oil to your guests as a gift for participating in the evening's ritual.

VII. Shadowlands

Psychopomps and their Talismans

Psychopomp	Origin	Talisman(s)
Ankou	Brittany	Scythe
Anubis	Egypt	Flail, fetish, jackal
Aumakua	Polynesia	Shark, owl
Charon	Greek	Coin, boat
Charun	Etruscan	Hammer
Epona	Celtic	Horse, cornucopia, grain
Freyja	Norse	Boar, falcon
Guédé	Vodun	Cigar, apple
Gwyn ap Nudd	Celtic	White stag, fairies
Hecate	Greek/Roman	Dog, torch
Hermes	Greek	Caduceus, rooster, tortoise
Horus	Egyptian	Wedjat eye
Manannán mac Lir	Celtic	Pigs
Mercury	Roman	Caduceus, lyre
Mithra	Persian	Bull
Morpheus	Greek	Poppy
Muut	Native American	Owl
Neith	Egyptian	Bow, crossed arrows
Odin	Norse	Raven
Thánatos	Greek	Poppy
Thoth	Egyptian	Moon disc
Volos (Veles)	Slavic	Cattle
Wōden	Anglo-Saxon	Beer
Xolotl	Aztec	Skeleton, dog, feet

Lustration or Bathing Washes

Preparation of the lustration or bathing waters can be achieved in either of these manners, or using a recipe of your choice:

Lavender Wash - Simmer together lavender flowers along with slices of fresh lime, for at least 3 minutes. Let cool and strain away all the solid material.

Rue Wash - Place equal portions of Rue and Vervain in a cauldron, and pour boiling water over this. Stir for 3 minutes, and then let it steep for another 3 minutes. Strain the solid material away.

Either of these washes can be prepared ahead of time, and bottled for their intended purpose, and to be carried to the funeral parlor, if that's where your ritual will take place.

VIII. Lunar Rituals

Lunar Goddesses

(*This list is by no means complete, but should give you clues to the amount of names available for use.*)
Aine, of the Irish.
Anahita, of Persia.
Aphrodite, of Greece and Cyprus.
Arawa, of the Suk and Pokot tribes in Kenya and Uganda.
Arianrhod, of Wales.
Artemis, of Greece.
Astarte, of Syria.
Astoreth, of Phoenicia.
Bendis, of Thrace.
Caelestis, of Carthage.
Cerridwen, of Wales.
Ch'ang-o, of China.
Circe, of Greece.
Coyolxauhqui, of the Aztec (Mexico).
Cytherea, of Rome.
Danu, of the Irish.
Diana, of Rome.
Dione, of Rome.
Hathor, of Egypt.
Hecate, pre-Grecian era.
Inanna, of Sumeria.
Ishtar, of Babylonia and Akkadia.
Isis, of Egypt.
Ixchel, of the Maya (Mexico).
Ixchup, Young Moon Goddess of the Maya (Mexico).
Kuu, of the Finnish-Ugrian realm.
Luna, of Rome.
Mama-Kilya, of Peru (Inca).
Marama, of Polynesia (Maori).
Mawu, of the Fon tribe in Benin.
Metsaka, of the Huichol Indians (Mexico).
Morrigan, of the Irish.
Nanna, Full Moon Goddess of Mesopotamia.

Ngami, of Africa.
Nikkal, of Syria.
Nsongo, of the Bangala, in Zaire.
Selene, of Greece.
Tanit, of Carthage.
Venus, of Rome.
Ya'china'ut, Moon Woman of Siberia.

Recipes for Moon Cakes

Moon Cakes I

1 cup finely-ground almonds
1 1/4 cups flour
1/2 cup confectioner's sugar
2 drops almond extract
1/2 cup butter, softened
1 egg yolk

Combine almonds, flour, sugar and extract until thoroughly mixed. With your hands, work in the butter and egg yolk until well-blended. Chill dough to make it workable.
Preheat oven to 325 degrees F.
Pinch off pieces of dough about the size of walnuts and flatten into rounds.
Place on greased sheets and bake for about 20 minutes. Let cool completely, then begin to coat with additional confectioner's sugar, coat after coat, until the cakes are nearly completely white with the sugar.
(If desired, you can make a simple white icing and coat the cooled cakes with that, instead.)

Moon Cakes II

1 1/2 cups all-purpose flour
3/4 cup confectioners' sugar
1/2 teaspoon salt
1/4 cup sweetened condensed milk
1/2 teaspoon vanilla extract
1/2 cup butter, softened
1 cup chopped walnuts

Sift together flour, 1/2 cup powdered sugar and salt. Stir in condensed milk, vanilla and soft butter. Blend well and fold in chopped nuts. Chill well.

Preheat oven to 375 degrees F. Line cookie sheets with foil.

Roll the dough pencil thin and cut into rounds. Arrange cookies on the cookie sheet.

Bake on top rack of the oven for 12 minutes until set, do not brown. Let the cookies cool on pan. While still warm roll the cookies in powdered sugar.

Index

Abbondanza!, 60
Barley Water Recipe, 200
Beltane Handfasting, 162
Calendimaggio, 29
Color Chart for Solstice Dancers, 193
Croning Ritual, 109
Dedication Ritual, 76
Drawing Down the Crone, 186
Fairy Wine Recipes, 199
Goddess Oil Recipe, 203
Handfasting, 147
Handfasting II, 156
House Blessing, 105
Il Viaggio delle Morte, 64
Initiation Ritual, 85
La Giornata della Dea, 51
La Vigilia, 3
L'ora d'Estate, 35
Lunar Goddesses, 206
Lunar Rituals, 178
Lupercalia, 14
Lustration/Bathing Waters Recipes, 205
Making Floral Garlands and Wreaths, 197
May Wines Recipes, 195
Memorial Service, 145
Moon Cakes Recipes, 208
Moon Trivia, 179
Music Suggestions (for Abbondanza!), 201
Phases of the Moon, 178
Primavera Giornata, 22
Psychopomps, 204
Rites of Passage, 74
Romancing the Moon, 180
Shadowfest, 70
Shadowlands, 141

Solar Rituals, 1
Suggested Decorations for May Tree, 196
Summerfest, 45
Welcome Ritual, 91
Wise Resolutions, 124
Witch's Tea, 118
Womantide, 132

Patricia Della-Piana's Bibliography

The Goddess Book of Psalms, soft cover:

There are 200 chapters of praise, petitions and incantations, which can be read as part of your daily personal devotions, for guidance or inspiration, and even used as part of your meditations. Consult this book at every sabbat celebration, to prepare for ritual and to focus your thoughts at those most important celebrations. ISBN 978-0-557-07976-6, © 2008, 80 pps.

Devotions for the Witch: Devozioni della Strega, soft cover:

Based upon the prayer books used in the Catholic tradition, dedicated to the female deity, here are prayers written on the occasions of childbirth, table graces, lullabies, along with historic works from ancient writers and newly-created pieces. Includes a calendar of events and a Litany of Martyrs, honoring those who were tortured or murdered in the name of witchcraft or heresy in Italy. ISBN 978-0-557-14575-1, © 2009, 228 pps.

Aradia: Gospel of the Witches, Retold, soft cover:

After 120 years, a complete and corrected translation of Charles Godfrey Leland's ground-breaking work. You will discover that some of the things we've always believed the book said, simply aren't in there. Be prepared to adjust your opinion of this most important book of modern witchcraft. ISBN 978-0-557-23479-0, © 2009, 246 pps.

Witch Daze: A perennial pagan calendar, soft cover:

A sourcebook of over 2000 pagan events, including some sort of pagan-affected event for each and every day of the year. You will find witchy or otherwise strange occurrences, holidays, incidents, occasions, murders, births, and much, much more. Space is provided for the reader to update additional circumstances, as they occur. ISBN 978-0-557-29698-9, © 2009, 500 pps.

Elemental Meditations, soft cover:

A collection of guided meditations that allow you to merge with the elements of creation, that you may better utilize them in your magical practice. These are lessons I taught years ago to all who wished to follow my path, and they incorporate virtually the same methods I used to understand and experience the elements myself, so many years ago. ISBN 978-0-557-72127-6, © 2010, 40 pps.

Voice of the Mother, soft cover:

A collection of messages, recorded while meditating on the Great Mother Goddess. ISBN 978-0-557-72142-9, © 2010, 192 pps.

Book Journal, soft cover, coil binding:

A book of blanks for you to complete, in which you may record Books you've loaned, Books you've borrowed, Your book wish list, Books you've ordered, and Your favorite books, which includes space for your personal review of those books. This book bears no ISBN number, and is only available through the Storefront, listed below.

All the above books are available through the author's Storefront at http://stores.lulu.com/deliathecrone Those with ISBN numbers are also available through Amazon.com.

Made in the USA
Middletown, DE
18 March 2021